Commercial Law Applied
Learn To Play The Game

Copyright © 2012
by
David E. Robinson

Edition, September 2012

Maine-Patriot.com
3 Linnell Circle
Brunswick, Maine 04011

http://maine-patriot.com

Commercial Law Applied
Learn To Play The Game
Contents

A matter must be expressed to be resolved.

1
Commercial Law

The principles, maxims and precepts of Commercial Law are eternal, unchanging and unchangeable. They are expressed in the Bible, both in the Old Testament and in the New.

The law of commerce -- unchanged for thousands of years -- forms the underlying foundation of all law on this planet; and for governments around the world. It is the law of nations, and of everything that human civilization is built upon.

This is why Commercial Law is so powerful.

When you operate at the level of Commercial Law, by these precepts, nothing that is of inferior statute can overturn or change it, or abrogate it, or meddle with it. It is the fundamental source of all authority, power and functional reality.

Commerical Law Applied

2
The Affidavit

Commerce consists of a mode of interacting and resolving disputes whereby all matters are executed under oath by sworn affidavit executed under the penalty of perjury as true, correct, and complete — on the basis of each party's commercial liability.

Such affidavit is required for an application for a driver's license, etc., or for certifying a document that the system desires a person to be obligated for. Such means of signing is an oath, or Commercial Affidavit, executed under the penalty of perjury as "true, correct, and complete."

In a court setting oral testimony is stated in judicial terms, sworn to be "the truth, the whole truth and nothing but the truth, so help me God."

In addition, the participant must verify and show the relevance of each assertion made to sustain credibility.

Commerce exists and functions without respect to courts or legal systems.

Commerce is both pre-judicial and non-judicial. Commerce is the economic extension of Natural Law into man's social world.

Maxim: "Truth is expressed in the form of an affidavit."

An affidavit is one's solemn expression of his truth. When you issue an affidavit you get the power of an affidavit. You also incur the liability involved.

An unrebutted affidavit becomes judgment in commerce. Proceedings consist of contests, or a dual, of commercial affidavits wherein the unrebutted points, remaining in the end, stand as truth to which judgment of law applies.

A claim can be satisfied only through (1) rebuttal by affidavit point by point; (2) resolution by jury; or (3) payment or performance of the claim.

Resolving the conflict or duel between Commercial Affidavits provides a clean basis for resolving disputes for "In commerce truth is sovereign". (Maxim of Law 3 of 10).

If truth were not sovereign in commerce — in all human inter-action and -relations — there would be no basis for anything. No basis for law and order, no basis no accountability, there would be no standards, no capacity to resolve anything.

It would mean that "anything goes", "each man for himself", and "nothing matters". This would be worse than the law of the jungle. In commerce, "to lie is to go against the mind."

Oriental proverb: "Of all that is good, sublimity is supreme."

Maxim: "If the plaintiff does not prove his case, the defendant (the accused) is absolved."

What the courts are adjudicating, and what government are ultimately making rules about, are these basic rules of Commercial Law.

No court and no judge can overturn or disregard or abrogate somebody's Affidavit of Truth. The only one who can rebut your Affidavit of Truth is the one who is adversely affected by it. It's his job, his right, his responsibility to speak for himself. To issue his own affidavit. No one can speak it or write it out for him.

Commercial Law maintains the commercial harmony, integrity, and continuity of society; "to maintain the peace and dignity of the State."

Over the millennia these principles have been discovered through experience and distilled and codified into these ten fundamental Maximums of Commercial Law.

There is no legal issue or dispute possible which is not a function of one or more of these principles. The entirety of the world's commerce now functions in accordance with the Uniform Commercial Code (UCC), the corporate United States' version of Commercial Law.

BIBLICAL SOURCE

1. *Exodus 20:15; Lev. 19:13; Mat. 10:10; Luke 10:7; II Tim. 2:6.*

2. *God's Law; Natural and Moral law; Exodus 21:23-25; Lev. 24: 17-21; Deut. 1:17, 19:21; Mat. 22:36-40; Luke 10:17; Col. 3:25.*

3. *Exodus 20:16; Ps. 117:2; John 8:32; II Cor. 13:8.*

4. *Lev. 5:4-5; Lev. 6:3-5; Lev. 19:11-13: Num. 30:2; Mat. 5:33; James 5:12.*

5. *1 Pet. 1:25; Heb. 6:13-15.*

6. *Heb. 6:16-17.*

7. *Heb. 4:16; Phil. 4:6; Eph. 6:19-21.*

8. *Book of Job; Mat. 10:22.*

9. *No willingness to sacrifice = no liability, responsibility, authority or measure of conviction; "nothing ventured nothing gained."*

10. *Gen. 2-3; Matthew 4; Revelation.*

10 MAXIMS OF LAW

1. A workman is worthy of his hire.

2. All men are equal under the law.

3. In commerce truth is sovereign.

4. Truth is expressed in the form of an affidavit.

5. An unrebutted affidavit stands as truth in commerce.

6. An unrebutted affidavit becomes judgement in commerce.

7. A matter must be expressed to be resolved.

8. He who leaves the field of battle first loses by default.

9. Sacrifice is the measure of credibility

10. A lien or claim can be satisfied only through rebuttal by affidavit point by point, by jury, or by payment or performance of the claim.

Commerical Law Applied

3

Re: The Maxims of Law

Maxim 1. A workman is worthy of his hire.

It is against equity for a freeman not to have the free disposition of his own property.

Maxim 2. All men are equal under the law.

God's Law - Moral and Natural Law. No one is above the law. This is founded on both Natural law and Moral law. This is binding on everyone. For someone to say or act as though he is "above the law" is insane.

This is the major insanity in the world today. Man continues to live, act, believe, and form systems, laws, and processes which presume to supercede and abrogate Natural or Moral Law.

But under commercial law, Natural and Moral Law are binding on everyone, and no one can escape it.

Commerce, by the law of nations, ought to be common, and not be converted into a monopoly of private gain of the few.

Maxim 3: In commerce truth is sovereign.

This is one of the most comforting maxims anyone could have for peace-of-mind and security, and one's capacity to triumph — to get one's remedy — in the business of life.

Truth is sovereign, and the Sovereign tells only the truth. *Your word is your bond.*

Maxim 4: Truth is expressed in the form of an affidavit.

In commerce, an affidavit must accompany and underlay the foundation of any commercial transaction. There is no valid commercial transaction without someone putting his neck on the line and stating, "this is true, correct, complete and not meant to mislead."

When you issue an affidavit, it is a two edged sword that cuts both ways. Someone must take responsibility for saying that it is a real situation. It may be called a true bill, as they refer to an affidavit in the Grand Jury.

Things may change by your affidavit which will affect people's lives. If what you say in an affidavit is not true, those who are adversely affected can come back against you with justifiable recourse because you have told a lie as if it were true. People depend on your affidavit; and are damaged and hurt because you lied.

Maxim 5: An unrebutted affidavit stands as truth in commerce.

Claims made in your affidavit, if not rebutted, emerge as the truth of the matter. Legal Maxim: *"He who does not deny when he can, admits."*

Maxim 6: An unrebutted affidavit becomes judgement in commerce.

An unrebutted affidavit leaves nothing left to resolve. Any proceeding consists of a contest, or duel without sword or gun, of affidavits wherein the points remaining unrebutted stand as truth, to which summary judgement applies.

Maxim 7: A matter must be expressed to be resolved.

No one can be assumed to be a mind reader. You have

to put your position our there. You have to state what the issue is, to have something to talk about and resolve. Legal Maxim: *"He who fails to assert his rights has none."*

Maxim 8: He who leaves the field of battle first loses by default.

Those who best understand and codified commercial law in the Western world are the Jews. They have had this Mosaic Law for more that 3500 years based on Babylonian commerce.

Governments exist to resolve disputes, conflicts, and truth — to be substitutes for dueling and battle fields so disputes and conflicts can be resolved peaceably, and reasonably instead of by violence. So people can have their disputes opened up and resolved before the public, instead of going out, marching ten paces, and turning to injure or kill. Legal Maxim: "He who does not repel a wrong when he can, occasions it"

Maxim 9: Sacrifice is the measure of credibility

A person must put himself on the line and take a stand regarding the matter at hand. One who is not damaged, put at risk, or willing to swear an oath on his commercial liability, cannot expect his issues to be resolved, for the truth of his statements and legitimacy of his actions have no basis, and he forfeits all credibility. Legal Maxim: *"He who bears the burden ought also to derive the benefit."*

Maxim 10: A lien or claim can be satisfied only through rebuttal by affidavit point by point, by jury, or by payment or performance of the claim.

In commerce, a lien or claim can be satisfied only in any one of three ways.

• By someone rebutting your affidavit, point by point, with an affidavit of his own, until the matter is resolved as to whose nonresolved affidavit is correct.

• By convening a Sheriff's common law jury, concerning a dispute involving a claim of more than $20, based on the 7th Amendment to the Constitution for the United States of America. Or you can use three disinterested parties to make judgment.

• By payment or performance of the lien.

Commercial Law designates the whole body of substantive jurisprudence, i.e. the Uniform Commercial Code, and the Truth in Lending Act, applicable to the rights and intercourse of persons engaged in commerce, trade or mercantile pursuits. — Blacks 6th.

4
Assessment

In commerce there is the Assessment aspect and the Collection aspect.

Assessment is who owes, and what, why, how and for what reasons.

The Collection aspect is based upon International commerce that has existed for more than 6000 years. The Collection aspect is based upon Jewish Law and the Jewish Grace period which is in units of three — three days, three weeks, and three months. This is why you get 90 day letters from the IRS.

Commercial proceedings are non-judicial. They are summary processes that are short, concise, and without a jury.

The IRS is the most active Commercial Collection Agency in the entire world, although the IRS is not registered to do business in any state.

Do you understand what you just read?

THE IRS IS NOT REGISTERED TO DO BUSINESS IN ANY STATE.

So how do they get all the money they get? Because you give it to them without demanding proof of their claim, or even if they are "licensed" to give you offers (bills) based on illegal "arbitrary" estimations.

THERE IS NO VALID ASSESSMENT.

The IRS cannot issue a valid assessment. The IRS has never issued a valid assessment lien of levy. It's not possible.

First of all, there would have to be paperwork, a True Bill in Commerce. There would have to be a sworn Affidavit by someone that an assessment is true, correct and complete, and not meant to deceive, which in commerce is, "the truth, the whole truth and nothing but the truth" in a court of law.

Now, nobody in the IRS is going to take commercial liability for exposing themselves to a lie and have a chance for people to come back at them with a True Bill in Commerce, a true accounting of their default.

This means that they would have to set forth the contract, the foundational instrument with your signature on it, in which you are in default, and list the goods and services that they have provided to you, which you owe them for — a statement of all the damages that you have caused them, for which you owe them something.

No one has ever received goods or any service from the IRS. The assessment phase of the IRS is non-existent; it is a complete fraud.

This is why the rules of Commercial Law come to our rescue. This is the beginning and this is the end; this closes the circle on the process.

5
The Crime

One reason by the super rich bankers and the super rich people in the world have been able to steal the world and subjugate and plunder it, and bankrupt it, and make chattel property out of most of us, is because they know and use the rules of Commercial Law, and we don't.

We don't know the rules, nor use them. We don't know what the game is. We don't know what to do to prevent the theft.

We don't know how to invoke and protect our rights, our remedies, and insist on recourse. We do everything under the sun except the one and only thing that is the solution.

No one is going to explain to you what and how this is happening to you. That will never happen. The powers-that-be will not divulge the rules of the game. They get away with fraud and steal everything from the people because no one knows what to do about the crime.

What CAN you do about it? WELL, YOU CAN ISSUE A COMMERCIAL AFFIDAVIT. You don't have to call it that, but that's what it is.

You can state in your affidavit that, "I have never been presented with any sworn affidavit that would provide validity to your assessment, and it's my understanding and belief that no such paperwork exists."

At the end of this document, you can put implicit demands upon them. Then you can state, "Should you consider my position in error, please respond within the next 10 days with your reasons why."

Now they have to come back with an affidavit that rebuts your affidavit point for point, which means that they have to provide the paper work with the real assessment, the true bill in commerce, the real sworn affidavits that would make their assessment or claims against you valid.

No agent or attorney of a fictitious entity can sign any affidavit for the corporation.

How can they swear as fact that the corporation has done or not done ANYTHING? They do not have legal standing. They cannot and never will provide you with this. This means that **your affidavit stands as truth in commerce.**

6
Enforcement

Go to all their laws, like Title 18, and tabulate the whole list of crimes committed against you in lying to you. This could be quite an impressive list.

If you tabulate the dollar amounts of the fines involved in these offenses, you could just take Title 18 section 241 alone, which is a $10,000.00 fine on any public official for each offense. This means that for every violation of the Constitution, or commercial law, there could be 30-40 of these just in Title 18. You're looking at $300 to $400 <u>thousand</u> dollars! When these start adding up, they become very impressive.

Now attach this criminal accounting to your affidavit and file it as a criminal complaint with the State Attorney. This is like putting the fox in charge of guarding the hen house but that doesn't matter.

Now attach your affidavit and criminal complaint to a commercial lien, because by their own laws, value system and penalties, they have hung themselves. When you lien them for those amounts, they can't come back and say: "Well, these are out of nowhere; they're unreasonable," because the came out of their own codes.

Now, take your commercial lien to the Secretary of State and file it as a UCC-1 Financing Statement. Then file this lien against every agent, individually. (The criminal complaint is optional).

They can't hide behind the corporate state, this fictional entity created by man to engage in perfidious actions which they could not otherwise do.

You can use this same collection process against the IRS just as the IRS uses it against you.

All the attorneys, judges, and the people who come against you, think this is a lot of gobble-de-gook, but they soon learn that your affidavit of truth is valid, and enforceable against them.

They will find that things become more and more uncomfortable with each passing day.

Even judges will think that this doesn't matter because they can get another judge to remove your paperwork against them. Agents who think they can hide behind the sovereign immunity of the government; behind all their power and prestige, all their attorneys and the capacity to get the courts to do whatever they wish, is going to save them. None of these have any effect on your process.

There is only one way that they can be relieved, and that is to come forth with their own affidavit that rebuts your affidavit point by point, and proves you wrong. If they should get this into court or before a jury, that's not going to do them any good because the same battle of affidavits still exists.

This means that the conflict between affidavits is now fought out in the open. And this is embarrassing to them because they are not going to change anything. This will simply do them more harm.

The only way for them to settle your claim is to pay it.

If they don't satisfy your claim you can give them a grace period, and at the end of 90 days, you can transform the Secretary of State into your Accounts Receivable Office.

Legal title to all their real and personal property has now passed to you. You can now file paperwork with the Secretary of State and serve this on the Sheriff and say, "I want to take possession of my property." Things then begin to get interesting.

If you send a criminal complaint regarding a public official to the Insurance Commissioner of the State, it becomes a lien against the official's bond, be he a district attorney or a judge, and he's dead; he cannot function without bonding. His bond in held in suspension until the issue is resolved.

All of a sudden we discover ourselves with what we've wanted all along; rules that pertain to remedy, with more power than they have because we are sovereign.

No one, not a judge, jury or anyone else, can overturn this process or change it. To do so would resolve the world into chaos. It would end all law and order and standards for civilization. It is not possible; they are stuck. This is the basis of their oath of office.

With their own process, we can use the rules of the game in OUR favor instead of being treated as slaves. This applies to everything and everyone; not just the government.

Governments don't have anything to support an affidavit of truth, or their actions. Governments invent all the regulations and statutes they impose upon you. No one is taking any liability or accountability. They may have some kind of bonding, but you can tabulate a simple traffic ticket into more bonding than they have, if you so choose.

Commerical Law Applied

7

The Commercial Lien

A commercial lien is a non-judicial claim or charge against a Lien Debtor for the payment of a debt or the discharge of a duty or obligation to perform.

A commercial lien has the effect of permanently seizing a debtor's property, in three months or (90) days, upon the failure of the lien debtor to rebut the Affidavit of Claim for the Lien.

The three-month delay in the execution of the lien allows for resolution of the claim either verbally, or in writing, or by jury trial, within the (90) day period of grace.

A Distress bonded by an affidavit of information becomes a finalized and matured commercial lien and an account receivable ninety (90) days from the date of filing.

The Lien Right of a Lien must be expressed in the form of an Affidavit sworn true, correct and complete, with positive identification of the Affiant. The swearing is based on one's own commercial liability.

A commercial lien differs from a true bill in commerce only in that ordinarily a true bill in commerce is private, whereas a lien is the same true bill publicly declared, and usually filed in the office of the Country Recorder, and, like all such declarations, when uncontested by point-for-point rebuttal of the affidavit, is a Security and an account receivable per 15 USC.

A commercial lien differs from non-commercial lien in that it contains a declaration of a one-to-one correspondence between an item or service purchased or offenses committed and a debt owed.

A commercial lien does not require a court process for its establishment. However, a commercial lien can be challenged via the 7th Amendment jury trial, but may not be removed by anyone except the Lien Claimant, or a jury trial properly constituted, convened, and concluded by due process of law.

A commercial lien cannot be removed by summary process, i.e. by a judges discretion.

A commercial lien, or distress, can exist in ordinary commerce without dependence on a judicial process, and is therefore not a common law instrument unless challenged in a court of common law, whereupon it converts to a common law lien.

A commercial lien must always contain an Affidavit in Support of Claim of Lien and cannot be removed without a complete rebuttal of the Lien Claimant's affidavit point-by-point, in order to overthrow the one-to-one correspondence of the commercial lien.

No common law process can remove a commercial lien unless that common law process guarantees and results in a complete rebuttal of the lien claimants Affidavit categorically and point-by-point in order to overthrow the one-to-one correspondence of the commercial lien.

8
The True Bill in Commerce

A true bill in commerce is a ledgering or bookkeeping/ accounting, with every entry established.

A true bill in commerce is your first Affidavit, certified and sworn on the responsible party's commercial liability as true, correct, and complete, not meant to mislead.

A true bill in commerce must contain a one-to-one correspondence between an item or service purchased, or offenses committed and the corresponding debt owed. This commercial relationship is what is known as "Just Compensation" (the 5th Amendment to the Constitution), in relationship between the Government and the American people.

A true bill in commerce is called a warrant (4th Amendment to the Constitution), and the direct taking of property by legislative act (e.g. IRS and the like), is called a "Bill of Pains and Penalties" (Constitution, Article 1, Section 10, Clause 1, and Article 1, Section 9, Clause 3 — "Bill of Attainder").

Commerical Law Applied

9
United States - US - U.S. - USA - America

"United States" - "US" - "U.S." - "USA" - "America" means: a federal corporation. — Title 28 USC Section 3002(5) Chapter 176.

The United States is a corporation. — 534 FEDERAL SUPPLEMENT 724.

It is well settled that "United States" *et al* is a corporation, originally incorporated February 21, 1871 under the name "District of Columbia." — 16 Stat. 419 Chapter 62.

The United States was reorganized June 11, 1878 and as a bankrupt organization per House Joint Resolution 192 on June 5, 1933. — Senate Report 93-549 and Executive Orders 6072, 6102, and 6246.

The United States is a de facto government, originally the ten square mile tract ceded by Maryland and Virginia comprising Washington, D.C., plus its possessions, territories, arsenals and forts.

As a corporation, the United States has no more authority to implement its laws against "we-the-people" than does the MacDonald Corporation, except for one thing — the contracts we've signed as surety for our strawman, with the United States and the Creditor Bankers.

These contracts that bind us together with the United States and the bankers are actually not with us, but with our

Learn To Play The Game   31

artificial entity, or as they term it, "person", which appears to be us but is spelled with ALL CAPITAL LETTERS.

All this was done under Vice Admiralty Courts.

Vice Admiralty Courts, in English law, are courts established in the Queen's possession beyond the seas, with jurisdiction over maritime causes, including those relating to prize.

The United States of America is lawfully the possession of the English Crown per original commercial joint venture agreement between the colonies and the Crown, and the Constitution, which brought all of the states, only, back under British ownership and rule.

The American people, however, had sovereign standing in law, independent to any connection to the states, or the Crown. This fact necessitated that the people be brought back, one at a time, under British Rule, and the commercial process was the method of choice in order to accomplish this task, first, through the 14th Amendment and then through the registration of our birth certificates and private property.

All courts in America today are Vice-Admiralty courts in the Crowns private commercial possession beyond the seas.

10
Redemption

The UNITED STATES defines the fictitious entity spelled like your name with upper case letters as a "corporation". The definition is in 15 USCA (United States Codes Annotated) Section 44:

> "Corporation shall be deemed to include any company, trust, so called Massachusetts trust, or association, incorporated or unincorporated, which is organized to carry on business for its own profit or that of its members."

The state has created this "unincorporated corporation" and has authority over it until you give them notice otherwise. This is what a UCC-1 Financing Statement does. It gives public notice that you, the secured party, have a claim against the debtor, the unincorporated corporation, known as your "strawman".

When you file this notice, you take this entity "out of the state", out of the jurisdiction of all fictitious entities into your private domain, your kingdom. The entity becomes "foreign" to the state, an unincorporated "foreign corporation" in reference to the state.

Financing Statement: A document setting forth a secured party's security interest in goods. The document is designed to *notify third parties* that there may be an enforceable security interest in the property of the debtor. It is evidence of the creation of a security interest, and is not itself a security agreement. It is filed by the security holder with the Secretary of State or similar public body, and as such becomes a public record.

Security Agreement: An agreement which creates or provides for a security interest between the debtor and a secured party (UCC-9 105(h)); an agreement granting to a creditor a security interest in personal property, perfected by possession or by filing financing statements in the proper public records.

Security interest: Interest in property obtained through a security agreement, which provides that the property may be sold on the interest holders default in order to satisfy the obligation for which the security interest is given. Often the word "lien" is used as a synonym for security interest, although lien most commonly refers only to interests providing security that are created by operation of law, not through an agreement between the debtor and creditor.

A security agreement must exist to file a UCC-1 Financing Statement but it does not have to be in writing or attached to the UCC-1. The security agreement may be a verbal agreement. Since your strawman corporation cannot speak, how can it write or sign its name?

In fact, you can still do all of the administrative procedures without filing a UCC-1 because you are the secured party and creditor nevertheless whether you file or not. Filing a UCC-1 is more for your benefit than for anyone else because it makes this subject more tangible to you and gives you confidence.

You can create a separation between you and your strawman if you wish by applying for a tradename for your strawman corporation to avoid the criticism that you are "contracting with yourself." Once this is filed, you will start receiving promotions in the mail advertising credit card machines that you can use in you "new business". You will not need to do this, but this indicates that the "corporate system" now recognizes your strawman as a "fictitious entity doing business for profit"; a corporation.

1. Go to the website of your state and apply for a Trade Name and a UCC-1 Financing Statement.

2. A security agreement is not necessary as this is a private agreement between you and your corporation; your strawman.

3. Put the HOSPITAL where you were born as the address for the debtor as this is where the corporation was created by the state.

4. List all of the contracts you have signed for your strawman, such as Drivers License, Social Security Card, Marriage License, Passport, etc.

5. Reserve a number that will become your POSTED REGISTERED TREASURY ACCOUNT. This account will be set up at the US Department of Treasury with the private man entitled US Secretary of Treasury.

It is important that you refer to this man by his name such as "Timothy Geithner", as you cannot deal with a fiction while in the private venue.

The number will consist of the registered number that is printed on the red registered mail sticker you get from the Post Office, plus your social security number with no dashes. Example: RR12345678US-111223333.

DEBTOR:

JOHN HENRY DOE, a Legal Entity
MAINE GENERAL HOSPITAL
PORTLAND, MAINE 04101

Organization Number: 123-45-6789

Secured Party:

John Henry Doe, a man
c/o 123 Main Street
Yarmouth, Maine 04096

Creditor Identification Number: 123456789

11
The United States is Bankrupt

America's been bankrupt since March 9, 1933 thanks to FDR's HJR 192.

Why is today's dollar worth two cents compared to a 1913 dollar? Why did FDR steal Americans' gold the following year? Why do Americans each allegedly owe $330,000 to the Federal Reserve today? Why are more and more Americans declaring bankruptcy today? Why is America becoming increasingly tyrannical? Why is the left-right dialectic fake? Why are foreclosures plaguing the country today? Why is privacy becoming non-existent? Why is America, as well as the rest of the world, a collectivist socialistic dictatorship?

The answers to these questions and more lie in James Traficant's speech to the House on March 17, 1993. This one speech is all you need, to understand the deep doo doo the world is now in.

The problem is that the Feds have taken over the country on behalf of the Federal Reserve. Thomas Jefferson warned about the dangers of allowing private banks, like the Fed, to issue the nation's money supply, yet that is what is happening today.

You can't pay for anything with debt; that is the scam in place now. With fractional reserve lending, the monetizing of debt, and the charging of interest, the debt will never be paid off.

Commerical Law Applied

12
James Traficant's
US Bankruptcy Speech

The Bankruptcy of The United States

United States Congressional Record, March 17, 1993 Vol. 33, page H-1303

Speaker-Rep. James Traficant, Jr. (Ohio) addressing the House:

"Mr. Speaker, we are here now in chapter 11. Members of Congress are official trustees presiding over the greatest reorganization of any Bankrupt entity in world history, the U.S. Government. We are setting forth hopefully, a blueprint for our future. There are some who say it is a coroner's report that will lead to our demise.

It is an established fact that the United States Federal Government has been dissolved by the Emergency Banking Act, March 9, 1933, 48 Stat. 1, Public Law 89-719; **declared by President Roosevelt, being bankrupt and insolvent.**

H.J.R. 192, 73rd Congress in session June 5, 1933 - **Joint Resolution To Suspend The Gold Standard and Abrogate The Gold Clause - dissolved the Sovereign Authority of the United States,** and the official capacities of all United States Governmental Offices, Officers, and Departments, **and is further evidence that the United States Federal Government exists today in name name only.**

The receivers of the United States Bankruptcy are the International Bankers, via the **United Nations,** the **World Bank** and the **International Monetary Fund.**

All United States Offices, Officials, and Departments are now operating within a de facto status in name only under **Emergency War Powers.** With the **Constitutional Republican form of Government now dissolved,** the receivers of the Bankruptcy have adopted **a new form of government for the United States.** This new form of government is known as a **Democracy,** being an established **Socialist/Communist order** under a new governor for America. This act was instituted and established by **transferring** and/or placing the **Office of the Secretary of Treasury** to that of the **Governor of the International Monetary Fund.**

Public Law 94-564, page 8, Section H.R. 13955 reads in part: **"The U.S. Secretary of Treasury receives no compensation for representing the United States."**

Gold and silver were such a powerful money during the founding of the united states of America, that the founding fathers declared that **only gold or silver coins can be "money" in America.**

Since gold and silver coinage were heavy and inconvenient for a lot of transactions, they were stored in banks and **a claim check** was issued as **a money substitute.** People traded their coupons as money, or "currency." **Currency is not money, but a money substitute.**

Redeemable currency must promise to pay a dollar equivalent in gold or silver money. Federal Reserve Notes

(FRNs) make no such promises, and are not "money."

A Federal Reserve Note is a **debt obligation of the federal United States government,** not "money." The federal United States government and the U.S. Congress were not and have never been authorized by the Constitution for the united states of America to issue currency of any kind, but only lawful money, gold and silver coin.

It is essential that we comprehend the distinction between real money and paper money substitute. One cannot get rich by accumulating money substitutes, one can only get deeper into debt. We the People no longer have any "money." **Most Americans have not been paid any "money" for a very long time, perhaps not in their entire life.** Now do you comprehend why you feel broke? Now, do you understand why you are "bankrupt," along with the rest of the country?

Federal Reserve Notes (FRNs) are unsigned checks written on a closed account. FRNs are an inflatable paper system designed to create debt through inflation (devaluation of currency). When ever there is an increase of the supply of a money substitute in the economy without a corresponding increase in the gold and silver backing, inflation occurs.

Inflation is an invisible form of taxation that irresponsible governments inflict on their citizens. The Federal Reserve Bank who controls the supply and movement of FRNs has everybody fooled. They have access to an unlimited supply of FRNs, paying only for the printing costs of what they need. **FRNs are nothing more than promissory notes** for U.S. Treasury securities (T-Bills) - **a promise to pay the debt to the Federal Reserve Bank.**

There is a fundamental difference between "paying" and "discharging" a debt. To pay a debt, you must pay with value or substance (i.e. gold, silver, barter or a commodity). With FRNs, you can only discharge a debt. You cannot pay a debt with a debt currency system. You cannot service a debt with a currency that has no backing in value or substance. No contract in Common law is valid unless it involves an exchange of "good & valuable consideration." **Unpayable debt transfers power and control to the sovereign power structure that has no interest in money, law, equity or justice because they have so much wealth already.** Their lust is for power and control. Since the inception of central banking, they have controlled the fates of nations.

The Federal Reserve System is based on the Canon law and the principles of sovereignty protected in the Constitution and the Bill of Rights. In fact, the international bankers used a "Canon Law Trust" as their model, adding stock and naming it a "Joint Stock Trust." The U.S. Congress had passed a law making it illegal for any legal "person" to duplicate a "Joint Stock Trust" in 1873. The Federal Reserve Act was legislated post-facto (to 1870), although post-facto laws are strictly forbidden by the Constitution. [1:9:3]

The Federal Reserve System is a sovereign power structure separate and distinct from the federal United States government. The Federal Reserve is a maritime lender, and/or maritime insurance underwriter to the federal United States operating exclusively under Admiralty/Maritime law. The lender or underwriter bears the risks, and the Maritime law compelling specific performance in paying the interest, or premiums are the same.

Assets of the debtor can also be hypothecated (to pledge something as a security without taking possession of it.) as security by the lender or underwriter. **The Federal Reserve Act stipulated that the interest on the debt was to be paid in gold. There was no stipulation in the Federal Reserve Act for ever paying the principle.**

Prior to 1913, most Americans owned clear, allodial title to property, free and clear of any liens or mortgages until the Federal Reserve Act (1913) **"Hypothecated" all property within the federal United States to the Board of Governors of the Federal Reserve, in which the Trustees (stockholders) held legal title.** The U.S. citizen (tenant, franchisee) was registered as a "beneficiary" of the trust via his/her birth certificate. **In 1933, the federal United States hypothecated all of the present and future properties, assets and labor of their "subjects," the 14th Amendment U.S. citizen, to the Federal Reserve System.**

In return, the Federal Reserve System agreed to **extend the federal United States corporation all the credit "money substitute" it needed.** Like any other debtor, the federal United States government had to assign collateral and security to their creditors as a condition of the loan. Since the federal United States didn't have any assets, **they assigned the private property of their "economic slaves", the U.S. citizens as collateral against the unpayable federal debt.** They also pledged the unincorporated federal territories, national parks forests, birth certificates, and nonprofit organizations, as collateral against the federal debt. All has already been transferred as payment to the international bankers.

Unwittingly, America has returned to its pre-American Revolution, feudal roots whereby all land is held by a sovereign and the common people had no rights to hold allodial title to property. **Once again, We the People are the tenants and sharecroppers renting our own property from a Sovereign in the guise of the Federal Reserve Bank.** We the people have exchanged one master for another.

This has been going on for over eighty years without the "informed knowledge" of the American people, without a voice protesting loud enough. Now it's easy to grasp why America is fundamentally bankrupt.

Why don't more people own their properties outright? Why are 90% of Americans mortgaged to the hilt and have little or no assets after all debts and liabilities have been paid? Why does it feel like you are working harder and harder and getting less and less?

We are reaping what has been sown, and the results of our harvest is a painful bankruptcy, and a foreclosure on American property, precious liberties, and a way of life. Few of our elected representatives in Washington, D.C. have dared to tell the truth. The federal United States is bankrupt. Our children will inherit this unpayable debt, and the tyranny to enforce paying it.

America has become completely bankrupt in world leadership, financial credit and its reputation for courage, vision and human rights. This is an undeclared economic war, bankruptcy, and economic slavery of the most corrupt order! Wake up America! Take back your Country." [emphasis added]

H.J.R. 192 - <u>Joint Resolution To Suspend The Gold Standard and Abrogate The Gold Clause</u> - dissolved the Sovereign Authority of the United States, and is further evidence that the United States Federal Government exists today in name name only.

Commerical Law Applied

13

The Power of Acceptance

The term "accept for value" is difficult to comprehend and understand when first encountered.

With this in mind, when you get a traffic ticket, a notice of a tax due, of whatever, one's first instinct is "Oh, No. I'm not going to 'accept' that!"

Why would anyone want to accept such a thing?

accept: to receive with approval with intent to retain. — Blacks 4th Edition.

acceptance: the taking and receiving of anything in good part, and as it were a tacit agreement to a proceeding part, which might have been defeated or avoided if such acceptance had not been made.

Nope! Not much better.

First, you have to know what the word "tacit" means.

tacit: something existing, inferred, or understood without being openly stated or expressed; something implied by silence; silent acquiescence as a tacit agreement; something silently understood. — Black's 4th, 1.

tacit: something done or made in silence; something implied or indicated but not actually expressed; something manifested without objection or contradiction; something inferred from the situation and circumstances in the absence of express matter.

If you accept the thing then there is an agreement; a contract. You agree with what is said (in writing or otherwise), whatever it may be.

If you don't accept it; if you don't say anything and remain silent — and do not object — then there is still agreement; a contract.

If you don't refute or contradict what they say (in writing or otherwise) there is agreement; a contract.

You certainly don't want to get into a court battle with anyone — no matter how right you think you are, what law you think is on your side, you always lose in any court.

So why would you want to "accept it (anything) for value"?

Well let's define a few more words and see if we can make any sense of all this.

conditional acceptance: an agreement to pay the draft (the bill) or accept the offer (of the draft or the bill) on the happening of a condition.

A "conditional acceptance" is a statement that the offeree (that's you) is willing to enter into a bargain (contract) differing in some respects from the one proposed in the original offer. A "conditional acceptance" is therefore a counter offer made in return.

Now the ball is back in *their* court. If they then do not answer they accept *your* offer by *tacit agreement* and you win!

power of acceptance: the capacity of the offeree (that's you), upon the acceptance of the terms of an offer, to create a binding contract.

So if you accept their offer, *with a conditional acceptance,* and put forth your terms upon which you DO accept their offer, you then now have a binding contract on your terms. The offeror — the municipality or corporation — must now come back with a rebuttal to prove your terms, or conditions in error, if they can.

If they cannot prove you wrong, or if they remain silent, the conditioned contract stands — and you win.

You need to accept the **offers of contract** that you receive, by claiming your control over the fictional entity (strawman) that the state created in your name when you were born.

In other words, "I am not the fictitious corporation (the strawman) addressed and stated on your claim."

Maxim 6: An unrebutted affidavit becomes judgement in commerce.

14
The Law of Presumption

"A presumption is a legal inference or assumption that a fact exists, based on the known or proven existence of some other fact or group of facts." — Black's 7th, page 1203.

Most presumptions are **rules of evidence** calling for a certain result in a given case unless the party adversely affected overcomes it with other evidence. A presumption shifts the burden of proof, or persuasion, to the opposing party who can then attempt to overcome the presumption.

The IRS makes presumptions about your status which are not true.

A resident of any of the 50 states of the Union who has ignorantly filed one or more IRS **1040 forms** in the past is **presumed by the IRS** to be an individual who is subject to the **individual income tax.**

Filed IRS **1040 forms** allow the IRS to presume that this individual was **required to file** or voluntarily **chose to be treated as a "taxpayer" who is required to file.**

The IRS is entitled to presume that this **nonresident** of the Federal Zone (the District of Columbia and its territorial possessions) has "volunteered" or is "volunteering" to become a "taxpayer" — an individual subject to the internal revenue tax — the tax internal to the Federal Zone.

The term **"presumption"** has a special meaning in law. A presumption is a **logical supposition** of a particular fact.

The Uniform Commercial Code (UCC) defines "presumption" this way at UCC Article 1, General Provisions, Part 2, Section 1-201. General Definitions:

(31) **"Presumption"** or **"presumed"** means that **the trier of fact must find the fact presumed until evidence is introduced to prove it untrue.** — UCC §1-201(31)

Black's Law, 6th defines "presumption" as follows:

A presumption is a rule of law by which a presumed fact exists as true until it is rebutted; a legal inference that operates in the absence of proof.

There are two opposite kinds of presumptions; **conclusive** and **rebuttable**.

A **conclusive presumption** is one for which available proof renders it so "conclusive" that it cannot be rebutted. To "rebut" a fact is to expose it as false ... to disprove it.

A **rebuttable presumption** is a one that can be disproved by sufficient proof. A rebuttable presumption is a lawyer's way of stating a fact that is really not a fact.

We are mainly interested in **rebuttable presumptions** because the Code of Federal Regulations makes certain presumptions about nonresident aliens of the Federal Zone.

26 CFR 1.871-4 - Proof of residence of aliens [of the Federal Zone].

(a) Rules of evidence. The following rules of evidence shall govern in determining whether or not an alien within the United States [Inc.] has acquired residence therein for purposes of the income tax.

(b) Nonresidence presumed. An alien, by reason of his alienage, is presumed to be a nonresident alien. [emphasis added]

Treasury regulations here are very clear about a key presumption that the IRS makes about aliens of the Federal Zone. Because of their "alienage" all aliens are presumed to be nonresident aliens.

This presumption is built into the law because the **Code of Federal Regulations** is considered to have the force of law. (Courts have ruled that the CFR is a supplement to the published **Federal Register** which puts the general public on actual notice.)

This presumption is a rebuttable presumption. The regulations establish the rules by which this presumption can be rebutted or disproved, as follows:

(C)(2) Other aliens. In the case of other [not departing] aliens, the presumption as to the alien's non-residence may be overcome by proof . . .

(i) That the alien has filed a declaration of his intention to become a citizen of the United States[Inc.] under the naturalization laws; or

(ii) That the alien has filed Form 1078 or its equivalent; or

(iii) Of acts and statements of the alien showing a definite intention to acquire residence in the United States[Inc.] or showing that his stay in the United

States[Inc.] has been of such an extended nature as to constitute him a resident.

— 26 CFR 1.871-4 —

Filing a declaration of intent to become a U.S.[Inc.] citizen will "rebut the presumption".

Acts or statements by aliens showing a **definite intent to acquire residence** will also "rebut the presumption". **Form 1078** is a Certificate of Alien Claiming Residence in the United States[Inc.]. The IRS Printed Product Catalog, Document 7130, describes this form as follows:

Form 1078. Certificate of Alien Claiming Residence in the United States

Who May File. A resident alien may file the original and one copy of this certificate with the withholding agent to claim the benefit of U.S.[Inc.] residence for income tax purposes.

Notice the explicit reference to "the benefit of U.S.[Inc.] residence for income tax purposes". What are the benefits of U.S.[Inc.] residence for income tax purposes?

The "benefits" of being under the protection of Congress and thereby subject to its exclusive jurisdiction. The actual scope of Social Security, for example, is limited to the federal zone, except for those outside the zone who wish to voluntarily partake of its "benefits".

Under the law of presumption, your use of a social security number can be treated by the federal government as proof that you have opted to receive benefits from the federal zone. **Form 1078** is ready-made for those who begin as nonresident aliens but later chose to declare themselves a "resident" in the United States[Inc.] in order to claim the benefit of that "residence".

Form 1078 declares a nonresident alien to be a "resident" for income tax purposes. **Form 1078** moves nonresident aliens into the jurisdiction of the Federal Zone.

There are other ways by which the presumed nonresidence of aliens can be rebutted or disproved by the IRS thereby moving them over into the Federal Zone.

For example, if nonresident aliens sign a **Form W-4** they are presumed to be **government employees** having income from a source inside the Federal Zone. Employers are to treat all employees as "residents" of the Federal Zone and withhold pay as if they (the employers) have not been instructed otherwise by the employees.

Notice how the presumption has shifted. Contrary to the regulations at **26 CFR 1.871-4** (quoted previously), employers are told by the IRS to make the opposite "presumption" about the residence of their employees, even if they are not true "employees" of the federal zone as that term is defined in the IRC.

If individuals have signed **W-4** and **W-2 forms**, the presumption is that they were required to sign these forms or they made the election to be treated as residents. Recall that the instructions for **Form 1040NR** describe the **"election to be taxed as a resident alien"**. This is accomplished by filing an income tax return on **Form 1040** or **1040A** and attaching a statement confirming the "election".

A very subtle indicator of one's status is the perjury oath found on IRS forms. Under Title 28 of the U.S.[Inc.] Codes, Section 1746, there are two different perjury oaths to which penalties attach: one **within the United States**[Inc.], and one **without the United States**[Inc.].

If an oath is executed **without the United States**[Inc.], it reads, **"I declare** (or certify, verify, or state) under penalty of perjury **under the laws of the United States of America** that the foregoing is true and correct.

If an oath is executed **within the United States**[Inc.], it reads, **"I declare** (or certify, verify, or state) under penalty of perjury **that the foregoing is true and correct.**

Thus, your signature under the latter oath can be presumed to mean that **you are already subject** to the jurisdiction of the United States[Inc.]. This latter oath is the one found on IRS **Form 1040.**

When you unknowingly rebut you status of being a non resident of the DISTRICT UNITED STATES by having filed one or more **1040 forms** in the past, **the filed 1040 forms do not cast the situation into concrete;** this presumption is rebuttable.

The IRS formulates the presumption from these filed forms that you are **an employee of the DISTRICT UNITED STATES** who is subject to the individual income tax and is required to file.

If you filed under the mistaken belief that you were required to file, that mistaken belief, in and of itself, does not turn you into a person who is required to file. Tax liability is not a matter of belief. (It's a matter of jurisdiction).

Tax liability is a matter of your status, and the jurisdiction in which you live, according to what you claim them to be.

Your best approach is to "clean the slate". In other words, clear the administrative record of any written documents which you may have filed in error or in the mistaken belief that you were required to file.

An **Affidavit of Rescission** can be used to clean the slate of constructive fraud that Congress and other federal officials have perpetrated on the American people.

Now, this law of presumption works both ways. You can use it to your advantage as can anyone else.

One of the most surprising discoveries made by the freedom movement in America concerns **the bank signature card.**

If you have a checking or savings account at a bank, you may remember being required to sign your name on several documents when you opened that account. One of these documents was **the bank signature card.**

You may have been told that the bank needed your signature to compare it with the signatures you would make on the checks you write, to detect forgeries. That explanation sounded reasonable, so you signed your name on **the bank signature card.**

What the bank officer probably did not tell you was that **you signed your name on a contract** whereby **you agreed to abide by all rules and regulations of the Secretary of the Treasury** [of Puerto Rico]. **Bank**

signature cards typically contain such a clause in the fine print.

These rules and regulations include, but are not limited to the **Internal Revenue Code** (IRC) (all 2,000 pages of it) and the **Code of Federal Regulations** (CFR) for the IRC.

These rules may also include every last word of the **Federal Reserve Act**, another gigantic statute.

Now, did the bank have all 8,000 pages of the **IRC** and its regulations on exhibit for you to examine upon request, **before you signed the card?**

Your bank should be willing to identify clearly what rules and regulations silently adhere to your signature.

You are presumed to be a person who knows how to read a contract before you sign your name to it; and once your wet ink signature is on the contract, the federal government presumes that you knew what you were agreeing to when you signed this contract.

Their presumption is that you entered into this contract **knowingly, voluntarily, and intentionally, because your signature is on the contract.**

Is this presumption rebuttable? You bet it is!

Here's why: Instead of telling you that the bank needed your signature **to catch forgeries,** imagine that the bank officer described **the bank signature card** as follows:

Your signature on this card would create a contract between you and the secretary of the Treasury [of Puerto Rico].

This Secretary is not the U.S. Secretary of the

Treasury of the United States, because the U.S. Treasury Department referred to on the bank signature card is a private corporation which has been set up to enforce private rules and regulations.

These rules and regulations have been established to discharge the bankruptcy of the federal government.

Your signature on this card would be taken to mean that you are volunteering to subject yourself to a foreign jurisdiction, to a municipal corporation, a municipal corporation known as the District of Columbia and its private offspring, the Federal Reserve System.

You would be accepting the benefits of limited liability offered to you by this private corporation for using their commercial paper, Federal Reserve Notes, to discharge your debts without the need for silver or gold.

By accepting these benefits, you would be admitting to the waiver of all rights guaranteed to you by the Constitution for the United States of America, because that Constitution cannot impair any obligations in the contract you would be entering by sighing this card.

Your waiver of these rights would be presumed to be voluntary, and as a result of knowingly intelligent acts done with sufficient awareness of the relevant circumstances and likely consequences, as explained by the supreme Court in the case of _Brady vs. U.S._

With your signature on this card, the Internal Revenue Service, _a collection agency for the Federal Reserve System,_ would be authorized to attach levies against any and all of your account balances in order to satisfy any unmade liabilities which the IRS determines to exist.

You would be waiving all rights against self-incrimination, and you would not be entitled to due process of law in federal administrative tribunals where the U.S. Constitution cannot be invoked to protect you, and where your home, papers and effects would not be secured against search and seizure.

Now, please sign this card here, for us.

15

The Law of Presumption Saves

How does the law of presumption help you in this situation with you bank card?

First of all, **you presumed that your signature was required to compare it with the signatures on checks you planned to write.** This was a reasonable presumption, because that's what the bank officer told you, **but *it is also a rebuttable presumption* because of what the fine print said.**

That fine print can be used to rebut your presumption, when push comes to shove in a court of law.

The federal government presumes that you knew what you were doing when you signed this contract.

Well did you? **Did the bank officer explain all the terms and conditions attached thereto as explained above?** Did you read all 8,000 pages of law and regulations before deciding to sign this contract? **Did you even know they existed?** Was your signature on this contract a **voluntary, intentional and knowingly intelligent act** done with sufficient **awareness of all its relevant consequences** and likely circumstances?

The Supreme Court has stated clearly that:

"**Waivers of Constitutional Rights not only must be voluntary, but must be knowingly intelligent acts done with sufficient awareness of the relevant circumstances and likely consequences.**" — *Brady vs United States*, 397 U.S. 742, 748 (1970).

Fortunately for you and me, the federal government's presumptions about you and me are also rebuttable. Why? Because the Feds are guilty of fraud by not disclosing the nature of the bankruptcy which they are using to envelope the American people, like an octopus, with a suction tentacle in everybody's wallet, adults and children alike.

The banks are unwitting parties to this fraud because the **Congress has a controlling interest in the banks through the FDIC (Federal Deposit Insurance Corporation)** and their traffic in **Federal Reserve Notes** and other commercial paper issued by the Federal Reserve banks, with the help of their agent, **the private Treasury Department** [of Puerto Rico].

Since this fraud can attach to your bank account(s) without your knowledge or consent, it is generally a good idea to **notify your bank(s), in writing, that the IRS cannot inspect any of your bank account records unless you specifically authorize such inspections by executing an IRS Form 6014.** The IRS Printed Products Catalog describes this form as follows:

Form 6014 Authorization — Access to Third Party Records for Internal Revenue Service Employees Authorization from Taxpayer to third party for IRS employees to examine records.

Make explicit reference to this Form in a routin your bank(s). Inform the appropriate bank officers must have a completed **Form 6014** on file \ authorized wet ink signature before they can legally allow any IRS employees to examine your bank accout records.

Then state, discretely, that you hereby reserve your fundamental right to withhold your authorized signature from Form 6014, because it would constitute a waiver of your 4th Amendment Rights to privacy, and no agency of government can compel you to waive any of your fundamental Rights such as those explicitly guaranteed by the 4th Amendment in the Constitution for the United States of America.

(Banks are chartered by the States in which they do business, and as such they are "agencies" of State government.)

You might also cite pertinent sections in your State Constitution, particularly if it mandates that the U.S. Constitution is the Supreme Law of the Land, as it does in the California Constitution of 1879.

Finally, you may wish to state that **Form 6014** does not apply to you anyway because you are not a "Taxpayer" as that term is defined by **Section 7701(a)(14)** of the Internal Revenue Code. Therefore, the bank is not authorized to release information about you to IRS employees, period!

Social Security is another example of a fraudulent contract with a built-in presumption.

Your signature on the **original application for Social Security,** the **SS-5 Form,** is presumed by the federal government to mean **that you knew what you were** etting into, namely, that you knew **it is voluntary**, that you knew **it isn't a true insurance program**, that you knew **it is instead a tax**, that you knew **Congress reserved to itself the authority to change its rules at any time**, and that you knew it makes you a **subject of Congress because you knowingly, intentionally and voluntarily chose to accept the "benefits" of this government program.**

Now ask yourself these questions:

How could you have known any of these things since nobody told you?

How could you have known since the real truth is systematically kept from you?

How could you have known, if all applicable terms and conditions were not disclosed to you before you joined the program? And how could you have made a capable, adult decision in this matter **when you signed the form as a minor, or when your parents signed the form for you?**

The answers to these questions are all the same: **there is just no way!**

For the record, Black's Law Dictionary, Sixth Edition, defines "fraud" as follows:

Fraud: an intentional perversion of truth for the purpose of inducing another (individual), in reliance upon it, to part with some valuable things belonging to him or to surrender a legal right.

A false representation of a matter of fact, whether by words or by conduct, by false or misleading allegations, or by concealment of that which should have been disclosed, which deceives and is intended to deceive another so that he shall act upon it to his legal injury."

The law with respect to fraud is crystal clear:

"Constructive fraud as well as actual fraud may be the basis of cancellation of an instrument." — *El Paso Natural Gas Co. vs Kysar Insurance Co.,* 605 Pacific 2d. 240 (1979).

Reverse these ominous presumptions which the federal government is entitled to make about the so-called contract you signed at your friendly local bank, or the contract you signed to apply for Social Security.

Commerical Law Applied

16

The Presumption of Innocence

A very effective technique to employ in a court hearing is to use the **presumption of innocence** doctrine to trap the judge into admitting...

(i) ...that the prosecutor has such a high burden of proof that he couldn't possible convict...

(ii) ...that the court is using prejudicial presumptions that destroy your sovereignty and rights.

Here is an example of a court dialogue between a defendant and the judge which demonstrates this technique:

1. Complete the form to indicate your plea; state that you are proposing a plea of guilty, but do not sign the form.

2. Wait in traffic court for your name to be called.

3. When your opportunity to be heard by the court occurs, follow the technique below.

<u>Court</u>: What is your plea?

<u>You</u>: Your honor, I propose a plea of guilty. I can't sign my plea form until I understand the charges completely and have had my rights read to me. I'm not a lawyer and I don't want a trial, but I'd like to understand the criminal charges against me and have them explained to me by the court. I'd like to avoid this whole thing. I have a life and a job and I'd like to get on with both. I don't understand all the ins and outs. As long as I can be fully informed, I'd be happy to pay your fine.

Court: OK. Well, what are your questions?

You: Am I entitled to a fair trial?

Court: Yes. Your are entitled to a fair trial. We're fair in this court.

You: That's great, your honor. Am I entitled to a meaningful hearing?

Court: Yes. Absolutely.

You: So if I ask questions, I can expect that you would be responsive?

Court: Yes.

You: If there is something I don't understand, you will do your best to explain it to me?

Court: Yes.

You: Great. Thank you. Am I presumed innocent of this alleged crime?

Court: Yes. Of course you are.

You: Well good. I'm presumed innocent. Am I presumed innocent *of every element of this alleged crime?*

Court: You're presumed innocent of the charge, move on!

The judge now has to be more specific and apply innocence to each fact that must be proved with evidence. He has already said that you are presumed innocent. Now he has to follow through with his part of the contract. The judge, however, usually won't be laughing because he is the one who must enforce the burden of proof you have just estab-

lished against the prosecutor. Other lawyers in the room might think, "How many elements do you think there are?" It's not your burden to know how many elements there are; that's the cop's and the prosecutor's job.

You: Well, your honor, no I can't move on. I don't understand. I need a response of Yes or No, sir. Am I presumed innocent of every element of this alleged crime?

At this point the judge will often turn red. He wants to impose his presumptions upon you but he can't do it now for you have created a tremendous burden of proof that will make it extremely labor intensive for him and the prosecutor to pick your pocket as a team.

Court: [gruffly] You are presumed innocent of the charge! Now, move on!

You: Sir, with all due respect, I can't move one. I need a response of Yes or No to my last question. Yes or no? Are you going to answer me or not? You said you would answer my questions.

At this point, the judge usually calls in security and will have you hauled out. This looks REALLY bad to observers in the court who are watching, because all you are doing is engaging in discovery and the court is violating your rights of discovery, and your right to a fair trial. He doesn't want others in the courtroom imitating this technique, and he doesn't want to make any more work for himself and the prosecutor than he has to. You have checkmated him into acting irrationally and denying you due process of law.

You have now set yourself free!

Commerical Law Applied

17

Clearing The Slate

AFFIDAVIT OF FOREIGN STATUS

This **Affidavit of Foreign Status** is a public notice to all interested parties concerning the Affiant's "birthrights" and his "status" as an "American Inhabitant" as that status would apply with respect to the American States (the 50 independent States of The Union) and with respect to the "United States" as follows:

1 • The undersigned Affiant was naturally born as a free Sovereign in [Affiant's State of Birth], which is one of the sovereign States of the Union of several States joined together comprising the Confederation known as the United States of America.

2 • The Affiant is, therefore, a "non-resident alien" individual residing in United States which entity obtains its exclusive legislative authority and jurisdiction from Article 1, Section 8, Clause 17, and Article 4, Section 3, Clause 2, of the Constitution for the United States of America.

3 • The Affiant's parents were sovereigns also; born in sovereign States of the Union.

4 • As the progeny of sovereign people, the Affiant was born, "...one of the sovereign people; a constituent member of the sovereignty synonymous with the people." _Scott v. Sanford,_ 19 How. 404.

5 • The Affiant is alien to a so-called "14th Amendment United States citizen" and non-resident to so-called "14th

Clearing The Slate

AFFIDAVIT OF FOREIGN STATUS

This **Affidavit of Foreign Status** is a public notice to all interested parties concerning the Affiant's "birthrights" and his "status" as an "American Inhabitant" as that status would apply with respect to the American States (the 50 independent States of The Union) and with respect to the "United States" as follows:

1 • The undersigned Affiant was naturally born as a free Sovereign in [Affiant's State of Birth], which is one of the sovereign States of the Union of several States joined together comprising the Confederation known as the United States of America.

2 • The Affiant is, therefore, a "non-resident alien" individual residing in United States which entity obtains its exclusive legislative authority and jurisdiction from Article 1, Section 8, Clause 17, and Article 4, Section 3, Clause 2, of the Constitution for the United States of America.

3 • The Affiant's parents were sovereigns also; born in sovereign States of the Union.

4 • As the progeny of sovereign people, the Affiant was born, "...one of the sovereign people; a constituent member of the sovereignty synonymous with the people." _Scott v. Sanford,_ 19 How. 404.

5 • The Affiant is alien to a so-called "14th Amendment United States citizen" and non-resident to so-called "14th

Amendment State residency, and therefore, he is a "non-resident alien" with respect to both.

6 • As a sovereign whose Citizenship originated in [Affiant's State of Birth] by birth, and who has remained intact in [Affiant's State of Birth] since then, the Affiant is also a foreigner (alien) with respect to the other 49 States of the Union and with respect to the corporate "United States".

7 • As a consequence of his birth the Affiant is an "American Inhabitant".

8 • The Affiant, to the best of his knowledge and belief, has not entered into any valid agreements of "voluntary servitude".

9 • The Affiant is a "non-resident alien" with respect to the "United States" as that term is defined and used within the Internal Revenue Code (IRC) (Title 26, United States Code) and title 27 and the rules and regulations promulgated thereunder as follows:

The Internal Revenue Code (Title 26, United States Code) and associated federal regulations, clearly and thoroughly make provision for Americans born and living within one of the 50 Sovereign States of America, to wit:

26 CFR 1.871-4 - Proof of residence of aliens [of the Federal Zone].

(a) Rules of evidence. The following rules of evidence shall govern in determining whether or not an alien within the United States [Inc.] has acquired residence therein for purposes of the income tax.

(b) Nonresidence presumed. An alien by reason of his alienage, is presumed to be a nonresident alien.

10 • The Affiant was not born or naturalized in the "United States", consequently he is not a "citizen of the United States" nor a "United States citizen", *as those terms are defined and used within the Internal Revenue Code (26 USC) and/ or Title 27 and the rules and regulations promulgated thereunder,* and therefore he is not subject to the limited, exclusive territorial or political jurisdiction and authority of the "United States" as defined.

The "United States" is definitive and specific when it defines one of its citizens, as follows:

26 CFR 1.1-1 - Income Tax on Individuals

(c) Who is a citizen. Every person born or naturalized in the United States and subject to its jurisdiction is a citizen.

11 • The Affiant is not a "citizen of the United States" nor a "United States citizen living abroad", *as those phrases are defined and used within the Internal Revenue Code (26 USC) and/or Title 27 and the rules and regulations promulgated thereunder.*

12 • The Affiant is not a "resident alien residing within the geographical boundaries of the United States", *as that phrase is defined and used within the Internal Revenue Code (26 USC) and/or Title 27 and the rules and regulations promulgated thereunder.*

13 • The Affiant is not a "United States person", a "domestic corporation", "estate", "trust", "fiduciary", or "partnership", *as those terms are defined and used within*

the Internal Revenue Code (26 USC) and/or Title 27 and the rules and regulations promulgated thereunder.

14 • The Affiant is not an "officer", "employee", or "elected official" of the "United States" or a "State" or of any political subdivision thereof, nor of the District of Columbia, nor of any agency or instrumentality of one or more of the foregoing, nor an "officer" of a "United States corporation", *as those terms are defined and used within the Internal Revenue Code (26 USC) and/or Title 27 and the rules and regulations promulgated thereunder.*

15 • The Affiant receives no "income with respect to employment" from any sources within the territorial jurisdiction of the "United States" and does not have an "office or other fixed place of business" within the "United States" from which the Affiant derives any "income" of "wages" as such, *as those terms and phrases are defined and used within the Internal Revenue Code (26 USC) and/ or Title 27 and the rules and regulations promulgated thereunder.*

16 • The Affiant has never engaged in the conduct of a "trade" or "business" within the "United States", nor does the Affiant receive any "income" or other remuneration effectively connected with the conduct of a "trade" or "business" within the "United States", *as those terms are defined and used within the Internal Revenue Code (26 USC) and/or Title 27 and the rules and regulations promulgated thereunder.*

17 • The Affiant receives no "income", "wages", "self-employment income" or "other remuneration" from sources within the "United States, *as those terms are defined and*

used within the Internal Revenue Code (26 USC) and/or Title 27 and the rules and regulations promulgated thereunder.

18 • All remuneration paid to the Affiant is for services rendered outside (without) the exclusive territorial, political and legislative jurisdiction and authority of the "United States".

19 • The Affiant has never had an "office" or "place of business" within the "United States", *as those terms are defined and used within the Internal Revenue Code (26 USC) and/or Title 27 and the rules and regulations promulgated thereunder.*

20 • The Affiant has never been a "United States employee", nor "employer", nor "employee" which also includes but is not limited to an employee" and/or "employer" for a "United States household", and/or "agricultural" activity, *as those terms are defined and used within the Internal Revenue Code (26 USC) and/or Title 27 and the rules and regulations promulgated thereunder.*

21 • The Affiant has never been involved in any "commerce" within the territorial jurisdiction of the "United States" which also includes but is not limited to "alcohol", "tobacco", and "firearms" and Title 16, Subtitle D and E excises and privileged occupations, *as those terms are defined and used within the Internal Revenue Code (26 USC) and/or Title 27 and the rules and regulations promulgated thereunder.*

22 • The Affiant has never been a "United States" "withholding agent *as those terms are defined and used within the Internal Revenue Code (26 USC) and/or Title*

27 and the rules and regulations promulgated thereunder.

23 • The Affiant has no liability for any type, kind, or class of Federal Income Tax in past years, and was and is entitled to a full and complete refund of any amounts withheld, because any liability asserted and amounts withheld were premised upon a mutual mistake or facts regarding the Affiant's status.

24 • The Affiant has never knowingly, intentionally, and voluntarily changed his Citizenship status nor has he ever knowingly, intentionally, and voluntarily elected to be treated as a "resident" of the "United States".

25 • The Affiant, to the best of his current knowledge, owes no "tax" of any type, class or kind to the "United States", *as those terms are defined and used within the Internal Revenue Code (26 USC) and/or Title 27 and the rules and regulations promulgated thereunder.*

26 • The Affiant anticipates no liability for any type, class or kind of federal income tax in the current year, because the Affiant does not intend to reside in the "United States", he does not intend to be treated as a "resident" or a "citizen" of the "United States", he is not and does not intend to be involved in the conduct of "trade" or "business" within the "United States, *as those terms are defined and used within the Internal Revenue Code (26 USC) and/or Title 27 and the rules and regulations promulgated thereunder.*

27 • The Affiant, by means or knowingly intelligent acts done with sufficient awareness of the relevant circumstances and consequences (Brady v. US, 397 US 742, 748 (1970)) never agreed or consented to be given a federal Social Security Number (SSN), same said as to a federal

Employee Identification Number (EIN) and therefore waives and releases from liability the "United States" and any State of the Union of 50 States, for any present or future benefits that the Affiant may be entitled to claim under the Old-Age Survivors and the Disability Insurance Act and/or the Federal Unemployment tax Act, which are and remain in force with respect to the artificial corporate entity established in his upper-case name.

28 • The Affiant makes no claim to any present or future benefits under any of the foregoing.

29 • The Affiant is a natural born free inhabitant on the land, and as such is a Sovereign Citizen/ Principal inhabiting the [the Affiant's local state] Republic.

30 • The Affiant is not "within the United States" but lawfully is "without the United States" (per Title 28, USC, Section 1746, Subsection 1), and therefore has no standing capacity to sign any tax form which displays the perjury clause pursuant to Title 28, Section 1746, Subsection 2.

PLEASE NOTE WELL: At no time will the Affiant construe any of the foregoing terms defined within the Internal Revenue Code, Title 16, United States Code, or within any of the other United State Codes, in a metaphorical sense. When terms are not words of art and are explicitly defined within the Code and/or within a Statute, the Affiant relies at all times upon the clear language of the terms as they are defined therein; **NO MORE and NO LESS**.

When ald to construction of the meaning of words, as used in the statute, is available, there certainly can be no "rule of law" which forbids its use however clear the words may appear on "superficial examination".

United States v. American Trucking Association, 310 US 534, 543, 544 (1939).

This sworn certification is being executed WITHOUT the "United States".

The undersigned Affiant below affirms under penalty of perjury under the laws of the United Sates of America that he executed the foregoing for the purpose and considerations herein expressed, in the capacity stated, and that the statements contained herein are true and correct to the best of his knowledge and belief.

_____[Affiant's autograph]_____

Citizen/Principal, by special appearance

in *Propria Persona* (*in my own person*)

proceeding **Sui Juris** (*of full age and capacity*

possessing full social and civil rights).

18
A Declaration of Freedom from the Tyranny of the Shadow World Government

An open Declaration to the US Federal Government.

To: The President of the United States, U.S. Senate, U.S. House of Representatives and US Supreme Court:

There comes a time in the affairs of humankind when it becomes necessary to throw off the yoke of tyranny which has insidiously taken over the governments of the world. That moment has arrived, as this still new millennium has ineluctably placed demands on We, The People, to stand in our own truth and take back our power. Herein lies the demands that We, The People, speak to power with indomitable conviction and undeterrable resolve.

We, The People of the USA, inaugurate this global civil enterprise through these uncompromising demands made directly to the Executive, Legislative and Judicial Branches of the United States Federal Government. As but a single collective representative of the world body politic, we implore the community of nations, and all peoples everywhere, to undertake this same endeavor wherever the need to break free from tyranny has become self-evident.

We, The People of these United States of America (USA), do solemnly take back our rights, liberties and powers, which are considered by all righteous governments to be inalienable, from an unlawful and tyrannical US Federal Government that has wrongfully and systematically encroached upon the inherent rights of its citizens.

We, The People, acknowledge the wrongful usurpation of powers, as well as jurisdictional and legal necessities originally possessed by the fifty Sovereign States of the USA. Through a longstanding pattern of legislation of unconstitutional law, these inherent powers have been unlawfully stripped from these Sovereign States. Each State is now fully empowered to retain their original sovereign status as established by the US Constitution.

We, The People, demand that the US Federal Government immediately cease and desist from legislating, executing and adjudicating all law which is not in strict compliance with natural law, common law and constitutional law. Furthermore, we demand an expeditious review of all US Federal Statutes in order to determine their fitness in this regard.

We, The People, demand that the US Federal Government immediately cease and desist from all illegal enforcement actions against its citizens, as well as citizens of other nations, which are in obvious contravention of international law, scriptural law, common law and US constitutional law. Toward this end, we demand the immediate closure of the extra-judicial detention facility in Guantanamo Bay, as well as the Parwan Detention Facility (formerly known as the Bagram Theater Internment Facility), and all others that operate outside the rubric of both the US Criminal Law Code and Uniform Code of Military Justice.

We, The People, demand an immediate and permanent suspension of each and every law, statute and rule/regulation that is in violation of divinely ordained human rights, civil rights, and constitutional rights. Especially where these rights are violated in the course of the repugnant state-sponsored administration of torture by the US Federal Government and its proxies in "safe" national havens around the world, we demand immediate termination of such inhumane and unacceptable conduct.

We, The People, demand an immediate cessation to all war-making activity around the world. This includes the immediate withdrawal of troops from the illegal and undeclared wars in Iraq, Afghanistan and Pakistan. This demand also includes the many wars being waged by proxy through covert agencies (CIA), as well as by all corporate, mercenary entities such as Wackenhut and Xe Services (Blackwater). The US Government will immediately end the illegal and abhorrent practices of rendition, as well as the extrajudicial killing of foreign citizens by drones and any other means utilized in foreign lands.

We, The People, further demand that all economic and financial warfare being waged against the perceived enemies of the USA be permanently ended. The relentless manipulation of the financial/economic markets of the world, to include equity, bond, commodity, real estate, derivative and currency, must cease without exception. Furthermore, the US Federal Reserve (privately owned, international crime syndicate) must be placed in a temporary receivorship, as its collection agency, the IRS, is dissolved and reconstituted as a lawful revenue-collecting entity in order to carry on the affairs of State.

We, The People, demand that the aerosol spraying of chemtrails in our skies, fluoridation of our water supplies, and the irradiation and chemical poisoning of our food be stopped. The EPA, FDA and NIH will be re-chartered, as will all other agencies and departments which have profoundly violated the public trust. The critical Departments of Homeland Security, Treasury, Energy and Interior will be subjected to an immediate review and reorganization in the interest that the People will be served first, not the corporatocracy which has been unduly enriched for many decades.

We,The People, demand a planned and orderly dissolution of the current US Federal Government. It has become apparent to all citizens, that there has been a multi-decade and ongoing pattern of illegal conduct throughout the executive, legislative and judicial branches of the US Government, which has been deemed to be in profound and fundamental violation of the US Constitution, as well as other foundational governing documents. Both the Public Trust and Social Contract have been irreversibly broken through this intractable and unlawful behavior, as the sacred Governing Documents of this once great nation have been left in tatters. We aim to see them restored to their rightful place and, over time, greatly improved upon to reflect the evolving realities and emerging needs of a rapidly changing world.

We, The People, demand the planned election and appointment of a law-abiding transitional US government, which will assume the proper, timely and thorough administration of all duties and responsibilities starting with strict compliance with the US Constitution and the Bill of Rights. This transitional government shall override all powers and perceived rights of governance which have been unlawfully arrogated unto the US Corporation and executed through the Uniform Commercial Code (UCC).

Finally, **We, The People**, demand that a TRUTH AND RECONCILIATION COMMISSION be established in order for the suppressed truths regarding all matters of State that have taken place without the People's knowledge and consent, and which have unduly put the American people at great risk and in substantial jeopardy, be given a full airing within the body politic.

We, The People, have spoken, and we expect a substantive response to these demands in the immediate future, whereupon the appropriate re-establishment of this Constitutional Republic may proceed forthwith. A national conference to discuss a Restore American Sovereignty Plan will be convened with all deliberate speed.

Commerical Law Applied

Appendix

Commerical Law Applied

1

"Failure to File" & "Taxes Owed"

Filing any document with the IRS is a voluntary act that overrides your 5th Amendment protection against "witness[ing] against [yourself], nor be[ing] deprived of life, liberty, or property, without due process of law..."

Know that there are two separate entities. The **"Internal Revenue"** and the **"Internal Revenue Service"** working together in concert.

The **"Internal Revenue"** is an agency of the government of the United States, and the **"Internal Revenue Service"** is a collection agency for the non-federal Federal Reserve Bank.

So when the IRS **"charges"** someone with **"willful failure to file"**, they are actually **"billing" the victim** for an income tax that the victim may or may not actually owe.

It's a presumption that needs to be quickly rebutted by the targeted victim.

The victim usually tries to fight the charge using the Constitution and/or Title 26 of the income tax Code without ever requesting a **verified assessment of the debt** under Title 15 of the Fair Debt Collections Practices Act. This gives the IRS the ability to be granted *a "nihil dicit" judgment* (*a "no response" judgment; silence is agreement*) in United States District Court against the victim, *making the bill a lawful bill.*

Once the bill is adjudged to be lawful, based on the presumption of a debt, the IRS gets to claim that the victim is fraudulently refusing to pay a legal debt and thereby converts the debt into a presumed criminal act.

If first you ask them to verify the so-called "debt" under Title 15, it forces them to deal with you as the "real person", not the corporate entity known as the "strawman". They have no jurisdiction over you from that point on, as the "real person", and you are then dealing with the IRS agent himself, and not the entire IRS corporation.

Respond to the case under Title 15 of the Fair Debt Collection Practices Act, and IRS agents have no jurisdiction over you, and the judge will treat them as they are, a collection agency, and NOT a government entity.

If you fight the case under Title 26 of the income tax code, the judge will think that you're crazy (but won't tell you why) because **Title 26 has nothing to do with the IRS**, it's specifically for the **Internal Revenue** instead.

2
"Tax Lien" list is now "Notice of Lien" list

From the June 1999 Idaho Observer:

Stevens County, Wash., alters lien language:
Auditor "tax lien list" becomes "notice of lien list"

COLVILLE-On March 30, 1999, Jim Shaver and a group of constitutionally-concerned Stevens County residents presented testimony before the county's board of commissioners in an effort to change the language of **the county's list of more than 2,000 IRS liens.**

The Stevens County Commissioners responded May 11, 1999, by advising Shaver by letter that, "The Board and the Auditor have read the materials you submitted and consulted with the County's legal advisor. It is our joint decision to **change the current 'Tax Lien' Index to a 'Notice of Lien' index.** This change has been implemented."

Stevens is a county of 38,000 people. **The IRS has placed liens on properties that would affect the lives of at least 19 percent of county residents.**

"The largest business in the world today, the IRS makes Microsoft look like a lemonade stand. The largest fiscal activity in the world today is the pillage and plunder of the American people," Shaver explained to his commissioners.

Shaver went on to explain how **the IRS, an agency that has been proven to be illegal, unconstitutional and**

which incessantly terrorizes innocent people in a manner that is totally lawless and discompassionate, has transferred all liability for its illegal property seizures over to county governments across the country. The liability has been placed particularly **upon the shoulders of the county auditor and the sheriff** because **the liens constitute unprosecuted securities frauds**, according to Shaver.

Shaver, who has been studying the IRS' use of this mechanism since the early 1990s, explained how **the federal collection agency (the IRS) uses the ignorance of county officials to create a seemingly "negotiable" instrument out of thin air.**

"The IRS uses the county to obey a state statute (RCW 60.68) that compels a county auditor to file a "notice" of lien in an alphabetical tax lien list.

"The IRS will contact the county auditor and direct him to add a name to the county's lien index. **Once an alleged lien has been added to the lien index, the next day the IRS agent can come in and say 'give me a certified copy of the lien index.'**

"Then he has proof of a spendable instrument to go out and pillage and plunder property," explained Shaver."

According to Shaver, such an arrangement **constitutes a securities fraud.**

The IRS is guilty of nothing because all it did was secure a certified copy of something that was obviously accomplished by the county auditor under state law when the lien was recorded, probably with a phone call.

From the certified copy of the lien index, **the IRS then creates a (fraudulently derived) "Notice of Levy" that is presented to the local sheriff.** The local sheriff is then told to seize the people's property and the sheriff then, dutifully, seizes the property and arranges to put the property up for auction. **"What the sheriff doesn't realize is that he is working from a notice. He is working from an <u>unperfected instrument</u>. He is working from a <u>securities fraud</u>,"** Shaver said.

Shaver is committed to shutting the fraud down. To prove to the county commissioners that **IRS tactics are indeed borne in fraud,** he explained how county officials should address IRS agents:

"OK, Mr. IRS agent...**in the past you have induced us into fraud that we won't be a part of any more.** Now, first we'll need **your delegation of authority from the secretary of the treasury of the United States of America to perform the assessment in the first place.** Then we want **your affidavit, signed and true, correct and complete, under penalties of perjury,** that this person owes something and whatever that amount might be.

"I don't think that they will be around because **the whole thing is a giant scam,"** said Shaver.

Shaver also explained that the affidavit is important because you positively ID the IRS agent and get his home address and business address in case you need to serve him.

After Shaver's presentation, the commissioners asked several very good questions that were answered by Shaver, with the authority of somebody that knows what he is talking about.

The information presented to the county commissioners was apparently compelling enough to convince them that **if IRS agents are going to use the county to create instruments whereby citizens are to have their property taken, then the IRS agent will just have to place his own freedom and his own assets on the line by submitting an affidavit.**

Ev Kytonen, one of the concerned Americans who supports Shaver's work and hopes that fairness and lawfulness will someday return to our embattled nation, said that this is just the first in a series of steps that shall be taken to educate Stevens County government as to its <u>County rights and responsibilities as the most powerful unit of government within our Constitutional Republic</u>.

This is a very important step in the process to educate county officials as to their true rights and responsibilities, under law, to protect the interests of its citizens from the tyrannical intentions of lawless federal agencies.

People from across the country who are interested in making a similar presentation to their own county commissioners are encouraged to contact The Idaho Observer at (208) 687-9441 so that we can put you in contact with Shaver.

— — —

The Idaho Observer   http://proliberty.com/observer/
P.O. Box 1353   Email: observer@dmi.net
Rathdrum, Idaho 83858-1353   Phone: 208-687-9441

3
26 USC 6331

This Section of Title 26 conveniently leaves out paragraph (a) — which says that <u>IRS levys can only be made against federal government employees</u>.

Neither a <u>lien</u> nor a <u>Notice of Levy</u> issued by the IRS are valid absent a validating <u>court order</u> signed by a magistrate!

If these forms have nothing but the name of IRS employees on them, they are a fraud!

The IRS often deceives financial institutions and county recorders into surrendering the property of taxpayers by issuing fraudulent "Notice of Levy" or "Lien" documents.

Fraudulent "Notices of Levy", printed on <u>IRS Form 668-A(c)(DO)</u> documents, quote portions of <u>26 USC 6331</u> but conveniently leave out paragraph (a), which specifically says that a levy can only occur against *employees of the federal government*.

The clerks of employers and financial institutions who receive these levies usually have no legal training and will just surrender the money or property of the accused without asking even a single question; on the mistaken presumption that these levies or Notices of Levy are legitimate. They won't even verify that the levy or lien is signed by a magistrate.

Oftentimes, they are threatened by the IRS with an audit, or levy, or seizure of their own property if they don't comply.

This weak link in our property rights is at the heart of how the IRS continues to successfully collect a tax that few

Americans actually owe. This unethical application of the tax laws is called *violation of due process,* and it is commonplace.

The federal courts, however, have said that the issue of a "Notice of Levy" does NOT constitute a valid levy. Below is one example:

A "levy" requires that property be brought into legal custody through seizure, actual or con-structive, levy being an absolute appropriation in law of property levied on, and mere notice of intent to levy is insufficient. *United States v. O'Dell, 6 Cir., 1947, 160 F.2d 304, 307.* Accordingly, in re *Holdsworth, D.C.N.J. 1953, 113 F.Supp. 878, 888; United States v. Aetna Life Ins. Co. of Hartford, Conn., D.C.Conn. 1942, 146 F.Supp. 30, 37,* Judge Hincks observed that **he could "find no statute which says that a mere notice shall constitute a 'levy'."**

There are cases which hold that **a warrant for distraint is necessary to constitute a levy.** *Givan v. Cripe, 7 Cir., 1951, 187 F.2d 225; United States v. O'Dell, supra.* The Court of Appeals for the Third Circuit state in its opinion, *221 F.2d at page 642,* **"These sections** [26 USC §§ 3690-3697] **require that a levy by a deputy collector be accompanied by warrants of distraint [issued by a judge in a legal proceeding]."** *In re Brokol Manufacturing Co., supra.*

4
Affidavit by Verified Declaration

To whom it may concern

WHEREAS the public record is the highest evidence form, I the undersigned, hereby create a public record in the jurisdiction of the Maine republic and the United States of America.

PLAIN STATEMENT OF FACTS

Fact 1: I have not seen nor been presented with any admissible evidence which demonstrates that the IRS is something other than <u>a collection agency for the non-federal Federal Reserve Bank</u>, and I believe that none exists.

Fact 2: I have not seen nor been presented with any admissible evidence which demonstrates that the IRS is something other than <u>a corporation incorporated in the State of Delaware in 1933</u>, and I believe that none exists.

Fact 3: I have not seen nor been presented with any admissible evidence which demonstrate that the IRS is something other than <u>a corporation unlawfully acting under color of law as a government agency</u>, and I believe that none exists.

Fact 4: I have not seen nor been presented with any admissible evidence which demonstrates <u>that the IRS is not required to adhere to Title 15 chapter 41 subchapter V § 1962</u>, and I believe that none exists.

UNDISPUTED CONCLUSIONS

<u>Title 15 USC Chapter 41</u> - Consumer Credit Protection - <u>Subchapter V</u> - Debt Collection Practices - § <u>1692</u> is an act of Congress designed to protect natural persons (1692a says that the term "consumer" means any **natural person** obligated or allegedly obligated to pay any debt) **from abusive collection agency practices.**

The IRS is incorporated in Delaware as a collection agency for a Puerto Rico Company: The Internal Revenue Tax and Audit Service (IRS), a for profit General Delaware Corporation, incorporated 07/12/33, File No. 0325720.

The IRS is not part of the United States government. — *Diversified Metal Products v. T-Bow Co. Trust, IRS 93-405-E-EJL.*

Several other Corporations involved with the IRS are also unlawfully acting under color of law as government agencies.

NOTICE

Notice to the agent is notice to the principal.

Notification of legal responsibility is the first essential of due process of law. — *Connally v. General Construction Co., 269 U.S. 385, 391.*

Your silence stands as consent and tacit approval to this regard. If no reply is delivered within 30 days you are agreeing to the foregoing and are legally estopped pursuant to: *Carmine v. Bowen, 64 A. 932, 1906,* **silence activates estoppel.**

I hereby reserve the right to make amendment to this

document as necessary in order that the truth may be ascertained and justly determined.

If any living body has information that will controvert and overcome this Declaration please advise me in writing by counter Declaration in affidavit form within 30 days from receipt thereof proving that this Affidavit is substantially false.

I, the undersigned, do herewith declare, state and say that I am competent by stating the matters set forth herein and that the contents are true, correct, complete, and admissible as evidence, and not misleading by my best knowledge and belief.

This document may be recorded and may be used at the discretion of its issuer under Rule 902 of the Federal Rules of Evidence including the jurisdiction of the State of Maine and the United States of America.

By my hand this ___ day of _____, 2012, [your name here].

Commerical Law Applied

5
Nil-dicit Judgment
("he says nothing" judgment)

The first rule of winning in court is to win before going to court. **The second rule** is to make the other party argue about something other than the case. IRS attorneys know this, so we should know this too.

The IRS is a debt collection service.

When the IRS charges someone with willful failure to file under civil law they are actually _billing the victim_ for a tax. The victim then tries to fight the IRS using the Constitution and/or Title 26 of the United States Code without ever asking for a _verified assessment_ of the debt under Title 15.

This _lack of request_ gives the IRS the ability to obtain a _nil-dicit judgment_ against the victim in UNITED STATES DISTRICT COURT, making the bill a lawful bill.

Once the bill is deemed lawful, the IRS gets to claim that the victim is fraudulently refusing to pay a legal debt, and converts the refusal to pay into some kind of criminal act.

Whereas in reality, since the IRS is a debt collection service for the non-federal Federal Reserve Bank, the victim can require that the IRS verify the assessment, _which the IRS cannot do,_ — and if it could, the victim could make the IRS take the action to the jurisdictional district the alleged debtor is in.

However the IRS cannot verify the alleged debt assessment; only the victim can do that by admitting the claim.

Going to court and arguing about taxes using Title 26 is ineffective for the following reasons:

1. Title 26 is used by the government to *determine* the tax.

2. The IRS is a debt collection service, not a government agency. *see Diversified Metal v. T-Bow Trust/IRS*

3. The bill issued by the U.S. Treasury *(under Title 26)* becomes a debt collect-able by the IRS *(which has to follow Title 15).*

4. If you fight the IRS under Title 26, you are fighting something they have nothing to do with. It's like contesting the electric bill to the mail man, he will just think you are a nag, and he can't do anything about it anyhow.

5. The bill has already been adjudicated under *nil-dicit judgment* and stands *if not contested under Title 15. You cannot contest the bill under Title 26 since that is the government code on how to figure the bill, not the bill itself.*

6. Demanding that the IRS verify the assessment *(the bill)* requires them to cease and desist *(under Title 15)* until they supply the documents.

7. The IRS cannot supply the requisite documents and therefore you have beat them before going to court. *see Rule 1.*

8. If you go to court you can argue the correct issue, *the bill,* not how they *determined* the bill nor its amount, thusly you can win by arguing the right point. *see rule 2.*

9. You can force the IRS to do the action in the judicial district *of the court nearest the debtor,* which they will not

do, therefore you won't go to court. *see YHWH's scriptures.*

Title 26 > Subtitle F > Chapter 76 > Subchapter A > Section 7408

§ 7408. Actions to enjoin specified conduct related to tax shelters and reportable transactions.

(d) Citizens and residents outside the United States

If any citizen or resident of the United States does not reside in, and does not have his principal place of business in, any United States judicial district, such citizen or resident shall be treated for purposes of this section as residing in the District of Columbia.

One of the common denominators of acquittals is that somewhere or somehow the victim did some type of request for assessment that was never affirmed.

This is diametrically opposite to all the victims who lost using Title 26 and the absence of applicability to the code.

In summary, just like a charge in a traffic ticket, don't fight the law and *their* reasoning, deny the bill and require them to prove that the bill exists as a matter of record, before they *make* it a matter of record under *nil-dicit judgment* because you didn't deny it.

Example:

A contractor (government under Title 26) issues you (contractee) a bill through their third party collection service (IRS), you do not respond. Third party collector service, whose actions and remedies are defined in Title 15, goes to court ex-parte and receives a nil-dicit judgment. You get dragged into a foreign court (USDC) and attempt to fight the contractor and their rules for issuing the bill under the Constitution and/or Title 26, neither of which applies, since it is the bill being discussed, not the entity that issued the bill or how said entity determined the amount. Any attorney would tell you that this is a waste of time. You (contractee) must first void the bill under the appropriate code (Title 15) and demand the case be kept in the proper jurisdiction (the nearest judicial district).

In essence, Title 26 applies to the government entity that determined the bill and Title 15 applies to the collection agency attacking you for payment. It's almost incomprehensible to believe that legally Title 26, THE INTERNAL REVENUE CODE has little to do with the INTERNAL REVENUE SERVICE. This appears to be a well orchestrated word-of-art trick.

6
Understanding Law

There are six basic types of law:

A. **public** law
B. **private** law
C. **corporate** law
D. **constitutional** law
E. **administrative** law
F. **criminal** law

And here's how they work:

The **INTERNAL REVENUE** (the **IR**) deals with the **INTERNAL REVENUE SERVICE** (the **IRS**) under **Administrative law (E)**. This allows the two separate entities to communicate with each other privately and off the record. They can do financial dealings without reporting them to the court or to the other parties. It also keeps those pesky human and Constitutional rights out of the case since **Administrative law (E)** is under the *executive* branch and not the *legislative* branch.

The IRS deals with an individual's strawman under **Administrative law (E)**. We want them to deal with us instead under **Private law (B)**, which will cause them to name and hold accountable the actual human being that is attacking you. But they created the strawman so they would not have to.

As long as you use Title 26 which is under **Administrative law (E)**, you are treated as a corporation (corporations don't have human or Constitutional rights). When you invoke Title 15, which deals with natural persons (which do have human and Constitutional rights) the IRS loses its authority because they will now be treated by the court as what they are, a private for profit Corporation.

Under **Private law (B)** you can deal directly with the human being and his real name, that is attacking you rather than the whole corporation. By dealing with the IRS under **Administrative law (E)**, you cannot invoke the natural person concept, since it is not included in its definitions.

Also, since **Administrative law (E)** is part of **Public law (A)**, any conviction can be moved to another section of **Public law (A)** called **Criminal law (F)**.

But, when dealing with the IRS under Title 15 you are considered a *natural person* and can invoke **Constitutional law (D)** if they try to violate your civil rights.

Remember, the IRS agents use pseudonyms to keep us from going into **Private law (B)**. A good rule to follow is if the IRS is trying to *stop it,* you should try and *start it.* **Private law (B)** cannot be moved to **Criminal law (F)** since they are under different legal concepts.

Summary

This is very, very important: If you invoke Title 26 you stay under **Administrative law (E)** and cannot use Constitutional and/or human rights as your defense since they do not exist in **Administrative law (E)**, which is for corporations.

The IRS has the authority under **Administrative law (E)** to move the proceedings to **Criminal law (F)** since both laws are relegated under **Public law (A)**. When you invoke Title 15 you move over to **private law (B)** and are considered to be a natural person, human being, who has Constitutional rights. Plus the IRS cannot move a case from

Private law (B), which is its own entity, to **Criminal** since that is under **Public law (A)**.

Definitions of laws:

In general terms, <u>public law</u> involves interrelations between the state and the general population, whereas <u>private law</u> involves interactions between private citizens.

Generally speaking, private law is the area of law in a society that affects the relationships between individuals or groups without the intervention of the state or government.

In many cases the public/private law distinction is confounded by laws that regulate private relations while having been passed by legislative enactment.

In some cases these public statutes are known as <u>laws of public order</u>, as private individuals do not have the right to break them, and any attempt to circumvent such laws is void as against public policy.

(A) Public law is the law governing the relationship between individuals (citizens, companies) and the state. Constitutional law, administrative law, and criminal law are sub-divisions of public law.

(B) Private law is that part of a legal system which is part of the *jus commune* that involves relationships between individuals, such as the law of contracts or torts, as it is called in the common law, and the law of obligations as it is called in civilian legal systems.

Private law is to be distinguished from public law, which deals with relationships between natural and artificial persons (i.e., individuals, business entities, non-profit organizations) and the state including regulatory statutes, penal law and other law that effects the public order.

(C) Corporate law refers to the law establishing separate legal entities known as the company or corporation and governs the most prevalent legal models for firms, for instance limited companies, Technically a company is a "juristic person" which has a separate legal identity from its shareholding members, and is ordinarily incorporated to undertake "commercial business".

(D) Constitutional law deals with the relationship between the state and individual, and the relationships between different branches of the state, such as the executive, the legislative, and the judiciary.

(E) Administrative law refers to the body of law which regulates <u>bureaucratic managerial procedures</u> and is administered by the executive branch of a government, and to the body of law that defines the powers of administrative agencies; rather than the judicial or legislative branches (if they are different in that particular jurisdiction).

This body of law regulates international trade, manufacturing, pollution, taxation, and the like. Also called <u>regulatory law</u>, it is the body of law that arises from the activities of administrative agencies of government.

Government agency action can include rulemaking, adjudication, or the enforcement of a specific regulatory agenda. Administrative law is considered a branch of public law. Administrative law expanded greatly during the twentieth century.

(F) Criminal law involves the state imposing sanctions for crimes committed by individuals so that society can achieve justice and a peaceable social order. This differs from Civil law in that civil actions are disputes between two parties that are not of significant public concern.

7

IRS Levys and Leins

Written By - Rico S. Giron, Future Sheriff of San Mahuel County, New Mexico. http://ricoforsheriff.com

The Federal Reserve Bank, a.k.a. the IRS, is the biggest lie and scam in world history.

IRS - are the three most frightening and loathed letters in the English language.

This deep-seated fear and loathing serves a very specific purpose. It serves to keep the People of America enslaved in submission to an illusion, a lie. It is an emotional and psychological chain around the neck of the American people.

The IRS has a horrible reputation and has earned every bit of it, it has by their own admissions committed crimes against innocent Citizens, and continues to be **the "Gestapo" of America today.**

They confiscate more homes, destroy more families, take more money, ruin more lives, and commit more crimes than all the street gangs combined.

They are indeed vivid proof that *"The greatest threat we face as a nation is our own Federal Government!"* — from "The County Sheriff: America's Last Hope", by author Richard Mack.

Here it is in a nutshell:

The IRS is a private, debt collection agency for the private banking system known as the Federal Reserve Bank.

Learn To Play The Game   107

The IRS is not a government agency. I repeat, the IRS is not a government agency. Never has been, never will be.

The IRS — formerly the Bureau of Internal Revenue (BIR) situated in, and with authority only in, the Philippine Islands (Trust Fund # 61) — later moved into Puerto Rico (Trust Fund # 62) as well.

In the 1950's, with the stroke of the pen, the BIR was transformed into the current, notorious IRS and brought onto the 50 united States.

This was done without any Congressional authority whatsoever. There is no Congressional authority for the IRS to exist and operate in the 50 states of the Union recorded anywhere in any law-books.

Again, keep in mind, that the IRS is the **"Private, debt collection agency for the private banking system known as the Federal Reserve Bank(s)"**.

Due to the naive ignorance of the American people, most Americans do not realize that **there are two titles 26.**

Title 26, Internal Revenue Code, is the **Debt Collection Manual** for the IRS.

This manual has nothing to do with Constitutional Rights. The IRS does not collect an **income tax**. The IRS is simply collecting a **user fee** payable to the Federal Reserve Bank because we Americans are using *its private credit system.* The **user fee** had to be disguised as an **income tax** to fool the American people and keep them enslaved.

Title 26, United States Code, is **non-positive law**, which means that no **American Citizen** is subject to it. However, all **U.S. citizens** *are subject to it.* In order to understand "**U.S. citizen**" you must go to **28 USC, Section 3002.**

Most **American Citizens** have perhaps *unknowingly,* but *voluntarily,* surrendered their sovereignty in exchange for the "immunities and privileges" of the 14th Amendment.

There are literally hundreds of silent, unilateral contracts by which American Citizens *declare themselves* to be **U.S. citizens** and thus subject to *both Titles 26.*

By *voluntarily* becoming a **U.S. citizen**, every **American Citizen** declares him/herself to be an **indentured servant** (a slave) to the non-federal, Federal Reserve Banking system **with no Constitutional Rights whatsoever.**

So then, Title 26, USC, is a *private law* that applies only to **U.S. corporate 'citizens'**, who are *all* employees of the corporate entity identified at **28 USC § 3002(15)(A)(B)(C)** as the United States.

(15) "United States" means—

(A) a Federal corporation;
(B) an agency, department, commission, board, or other entity of the United States; or
(C) an instrumentality of the United States.

Consider this fact.

When an IRS agent wants to seize property from a Citizen in a County, they must first contact the Sheriff of the County and request assistance in the seizure because the IRS agent has no authority to seize any property at all.

So the IRS agent bamboozles the Sheriff into committing the crime, *for the IRS.*

When the Sheriff seizes property from a Citizen under the *non-authority* of the IRS agent, the Sheriff has committed a Second Degree Felony, *Conversion of Property.*

A second degree felony is incredibly serious!

However, both the IRS agent and the Sheriff, knowingly or unknowingly, count on the ignorance of the Citizen who has no idea what their Lawful Rights are.

Bear this point in mind: If the IRS agent has no authority to seize any property at all, then they cannot *delegate,* or *confer* to the Sheriff what they do not have.

In addition, the Sheriff has no idea that he has engaged in a serious crime.

Here is where the maxim, *"**Ignorance of the law is no excuse** [for violating the law]"* applies. Hence the maxim, *"**The Law leaves the wrong-doer where it finds him**".*

We do not have an excuse based on the legal system. Both the IRS agent and the Sheriff should be arrested and charged with **"Conversion of property"**, a second degree felony.

Tyranny is defined as: *"Dominance through threat of punishment and violence, oppressive rule, abusive government, cruelty and injustice."*

What better definition than this fits the abusive IRS.

America is using a ***private credit system*** wherein the medium of exchange is the Federal Reserve Notes that we call "Dollars". Hence, the so-called "Income Tax" is in reality nothing more than a disguised "User Fee" that Americans must pay to the non-federal, Federal Reserve Bank for *using* their private credit system. — [research Title 12, USC].

The legal definition of "dollar" is *"a gold or silver coin of a **specific weight** and with **specific markings**".* Thus, a Federal Reserve Note (FRN), is not and cannot ever be, a dollar. A Note is not "money". — [see Blacks Law Dictionary].

The Federal Reserve Notes in use today are mere *evidence of a debt.* I repeat for emphasis, Federal Reserve Notes are not dollars and can never be dollars.

The Federal Reserve Banking system is not a Federal government agency, there aren't "reserves" and there is no real *"money of account of the United States"* in existence and use to day.

The Federal Reserve Banking system is a **private cartel** that has usurped the authority of the Congress to coin Money.

Federal Reserve Notes are just as worthless or just as valuable as Monopoly Money used in the game "Monopoly".

If we go to the "Constitution for the united States of America", Article I, section 8, we find that only Congress was given the authority ***"To coin money, regulate the Value thereof, and of foreign Coin, and fix the Standard of Weights and Measures".***

This authority given to Congress by the "Constitution for the united States of America" was not to be delegated to any private corporation for that corporation's private gain.

The authority to coin money was usurped by the unlawful enactment of the Federal Reserve Act of 1913. The Federal Reserve Act is a "private law" passed by only four congressmen after the congressional session had closed for the Christmas holiday in December of 1913.

Congress can pass both private laws and public laws. congress does not have to tell the American Citizens which law is private and which law is public.

We are simply led to believe that all laws are public. This

is propaganda and brainwashing at its best.

Starting from 1913, we Americans *voluntarily* submitted to this private law through our own ignorance. Once we submitted to this "private contract law" we became voluntary slaves of the Federal Reserve System.

This was a silent **coup d'e-tat** wherein the American People became the slaves of the Federal Reserve Bank.

The "Killing Blow", the **coup de grace** *[pronounced, de gra]* was delivered upon the American People by Franklin D. Roosevelt in 1933 by removing the Gold Standard from the American economy.

Franklin Roosevelt assisted the FRB in heisting the gold supply from this country right out from under our noses.

The Federal Reserve Bank is the single largest **sting operation** ever set in motion. FDR knew what he was doing.

Since then, no American Citizen has actually "paid" for anything, we have just exchanged worthless Federal Reserved Notes for more worthless Federal Reserve Notes.

We **lease** our property from the STATE OF [your STATE], we lease our cars, we lease our houses, **WE OWN NOTHING!**

Since 1933 no American has owned their property in allodium. That is why the "STATE OF [your STATE]" can take your property for just about any reason, i.e eminent domain, failure to pay so-called **property taxes, state income tax, etc.**

For anyone who has ever dealt with a debt collection agency, you know how nasty, mean and dirty they can be. Now, take that nastiness, that mean-ness and dirtiness and multiply it one hundred fold, there you have the attitude the IRS.

Let's continue down the Rabbit Hole.

When an American Citizen gets into a dispute with the IRS, the IRS agent will not listen to any of your pleadings, your begging or your excuses.

Everything you do or say amounts to nothing with the IRS. If you dig in your heels and refuse to pay, the IRS starts sending you threatening letters with dire consequences and fines for your non-cooperation.

If you still refuse to pay, the IRS will file a document called a **Notice of Federal Tax Lien** in the local County Clerk's office. This is a deceptive document. Keep one thing in mind a **Notice** is not the **Lien** itself. The "Lien" is a totally separate and distinct document from the "Notice".

The County Clerk, through ignorance files the **Notice of Federal Tax Lien** as if it was an actual **Lien**. These are two separate and distinct documents.

The County Clerk never requests the actual "Lien" from the IRS agent. If they were to request this document, the IRS agent would get very irate and threaten the County Clerk for their non-cooperation. The actual **Lien** does not exist.

There is one more lawful requirement that the County Clerk must comply with before they can file the **Notice of Federal Tax Lien** or the actual **Lien** itself, that does not exist.

The Federal Lien Registration Act requires **Certification of a Lien** itself. This would require that the IRS agent file an Affidavit wherein they identify themselves, and state under Oath that there is an actual **Lien** filed against the particular

_... the County Clerk fails to verify **"Certification"** they violate the lawful requirements of the Federal Lien Registration Act.

The IRS never files the actual **Lien** because it does not exist.

An actual **Lien** must be based on a lawful assessment documented on **Form 23C**. In the entire history of the IRS, the IRS has never produced a **Form 23C** showing an individual assessment against an American Citizen.

This so-called **Notice of Federal Tax Lien** is an act of **Financial Terrorism** because once this mere **Notice** is filed, you become a pariah, a financial outcast, you are branded as unfit, you are no longer a good **slave**, you are a rebel beyond the hope of redemption. Your slave **Credit Rating** takes a nosedive. You are practically ruined financially.

Interestingly, **Section 803** of the so-called **PATRIOT ACT** defines **terrorism** as *"any act intended to coerce or threaten a civilian population"*.

So by the very definition of **Terrorism**, the IRS is the largest, meanest, dirtiest, Terrorist Organization in the entire world.

However, the so called **government** has exempted itself, its political subdivisions, and all federal corporate officers from being charged with **terrorism** under **Section 803**. Pretty convenient, huh!

If you still are not intimidated, the IRS will file a **Notice of Levy** with the County Clerk, and send copies to your employer and bank(s). The County Clerk, through ignorance, files the **Notice of Levy** as if it were an actual **Levy**, and this makes it so. Whereas these were two separate and distinct documents.

Again, keep in mind, a **Notice** is not a **Levy**. On the basis of this **Notice** alone, the bank then hands over all of your money to the IRS, and you cannot even pay your bills.

Your employer garnishes your paycheck, and again, you are the slave of the Federal Reserve Bank.

Your Bank treats the **Notice of Levy** as if it were an actual **Levy**. Your employer also treats the **Notice of Levy** as if it were an actual **Levy**. The bank and your employer never request *an actual copy* of the **Levy** itself. Of course, the actual **Levy** does not exist.

There are several things wrong with these two scenarios. Both the bank and your employer fail to verify several key pieces of information in dealing with the IRS agent.

First, they fail to ask for a copy of the IRS agent's **drivers license** to verify that in fact they are who they say they are, and in case the IRS agent has to be served with legal process, so they can be located.

All IRS agents have been given instructions to never provide this information to any one asking for it. Thus, the true Identity of the IRS agent is never established. Pretty convenient, huh!

Second, the bank and your employer fail to request a copy of the **Pocket Commission** from the IRS agent. Every IRS agent receives what is called a **Pocket Commission**. This **Pocket Commission** identifies the IRS agent's authority as to his/her actions.

The most common type of **Pocket Commission** is what is called **Administrative**. This is identified with a capital "**A**" on their identity card. This means that this IRS agent can shuffle paperwork all day, but he/she does not have any "Enforcement" authority whatsoever.

The other type of "Pocket Commission" is what is called **Enforcement**. The word **"Enforcement"** might convey the message that this IRS agent actually has unlimited authority to **Enforce** something against American Citizens. This is not the case at all. They have an extremely limited scope of authority. In fact, they cannot enforce anything against American Citizens.

Both the bank and your employer fail to request a copy of the **Pocket Commission** from the IRS agent in order to establish the basis for the authority of the IRS agent.

I am fairly confident that all agents that send out notices to banks and employers have an **Administrative** ("A" type) **Pocket Commission**. Thus, both your bank and your employer *steal your money* and send it to a Terrorist Agency known as the IRS.

Thirdly, the bank and your employer fail to request a copy of the **actual assessment** documented on **Form 23C**. Again, never in the history of this country has an American Citizen been assessed an Income Tax on a **Form 23C**. Without this so-called assessment on this specific form, **Form 23C**, there is no debt.

So the bank and your employer fail to verify this alleged debt and thus, steal your money.

Fourth, the bank and your employer fail to request of copy of the **Abstract of Court Judgment**. This document would show that you were actually sued by the IRS and that you had your day in court. **The 7th Amendment** of the Bill of Rights of the Constitution for the united States of America **guarantees you "the right of trial by Jury" in any controversy where the amount shall exceed $20 dollars.**

Of course, you were never sued and you never had your day in court. Thus your **Due Process of Law Rights** are totally violated, and again you are further enslaved to the Federal Reserve Bank.

So then, we come to the end of the Rabbit Hole. **You have never owed any money to the IRS.** The IRS is simply the enforcer, the debt collector for the Federal Reserve Banking System.

However, because you are using *a private credit system,* wherein the medium of exchange are fancy pieces of paper called Federal Reserve Notes, you owe the Federal Reserve Bank a **"user fee".**

By way of information, the IRS does not have a bank account wherein your tax payments **(user fees)** are deposited. All of your tax payments are deposited into the bank account of the Federal Reserve Bank in one region or another.

"The Federal Reserve Banks and the IRS constitute the single largest sting operation, the single largest fraud and the single largest swindle in the history of the World."

In order to keep this **Alice in Wonderland** illusion going, the so-called **government** developed an entire industry to support and perpetuate this fraud. **The tax preparation industry.**

Tax preparers, accountants, so-called Certified Public Accountants, self proclaimed financial gurus advising about tax loopholes, etc., etc.

All the current paycheck garnishments in the entire country could be stopped by having your employer request the above mentioned documents, to wit:

1. A copy of the **Driver's License** of the IRS agent;

2. A copy of the **Pocket Commission** showing the authority of the IRS agent;

3. A copy of the **assessment** against the American Citizen shown on **Form 23C;**

4. A copy of the **Abstract of Court Judgment** that verifies that you had a trial by jury.

As Sheriff of San Miguel County, I will provide **educational classes t**o the County Clerk and the employers who are currently garnishing wages and paychecks to identify areas where they may have broken the law and unwittingly stolen their employees Federal Reserve Notes and thus committed **Conversion of Property — a second degree felony.**

Furthermore, I will work closely with the County Clerk through **education and knowledge** so that the County Clerk can stop breaking the law and committing financial terrorism against the Citizens of San Miguel County.

When the Citizens of San Miguel County elect me as their new Sheriff in town, _I will ban the IRS from San Miguel County_ — and if I catch an IRS agent within the boundaries of the county _without my permission,_ I will arrest him for TRESPASSING!

IRS Strategy

The IRS operates a clearly defined and very clever scam. Here is how it works.

(1) The IRS **presumes** a fictional, fraudulent, nebulous, libelous and imaginary assessment against a citizen.

(2) The IRS **presents** this assessment as a Notice of Tax Lien to the County Recorder.

(3) A **Notice of Tax Lien** is supposed to instruct the tax "debtor" as to where the actual Tax Lien can be found, studied, and copied so that it can be challenged if necessary, but the Notice of Tax Lien never does provide that information because the IRS never produces any Tax Liens to which a Notice could refer.

(4) An unlawful statute injected into the Revised Code of Washington at **RCW 60.68.045** by the IRS, and uncritically allowed to reside there by legislators, other officers of the government, and citizens, directs the County Recorder to enter the **Notice of Tax Lien** on a **Tax Lien" Index**.

(5) But a **Notice of Tax Lien** does not contain a sworn (affidavit) assessment and is therefore only a non-negotiable/nonspendable paper instrument, which means that it cannot be used as money after maturing unchallenged 90 days, to procure, seize and sell property.

(6) And a Lien, any lien, if lawfully constructed must contain **a sworn** (by affidavit) **assessment** as part of the full disclosure requirement of all negotiable instruments, and is

therefore a negotiable/spendable paper instrument, which means that it can be used as money after maturing unchallenged for 90 days, to procure, seize and sell property.

(7) Since the IRS never presents a Tax Lien to the County Recorder, because IRS agents do not want the liability for presenting a false, fraudulent, nebulous, and/or libelous assessment, it must procure **or suborn** the County Recorder to do IRS counterfeiting for it by counterfeiting the **appearance** of the existence of a Tax Lien by **changing** the title from a **Notice** into a **Lien** by unlawfully entering it on the wrong **Index**, a **Tax Lien Index**.

(8) By changing the title from a **Notice** into a **Lien**, the County Recorder has converted a non-negotiable/non-spendable paper into a negotiable/spendable ledger entry, and has therefore counterfeited a currency, for the IRS, lacking full disclosure.

(9) Then, all the IRS has to do is to ask the County Recorder for a Certified Copy of the **Tax Lien Index** to **prove** that a Lien has been filed. This **Certified Copy** of the **Tax Lien Index** has the same power in commerce as a Federal Reserve Note because it can be used as money to procure, seize and sell property, to transfer property from the citizens to the IRS.

(10) Once the IRS has the Certified Copy of the **Tax Lien Index** implying the filing of a Lien, the IRS can begin taking wages, bank accounts, investments, social security payments, retirement benefits, houses, cars, and just about anything else that will bring cash to the IRS directly or by auction.

(11) The Public, the Legal Establishment, and the Courts, are all conditioned by threats of IRS retaliation to do

whatever the IRS dictates, so the scam is complete. Therefore, there is no remedy through the judicial courts.

The ONLY REMEDY of this problem is to ignore the judicial system and to use the same ancient and timeless system of commerce which the IRS uses, but to use the commercial system lawfully and properly **by doing everything with sworn affidavits containing full disclosure** (Exodus 20:16).

Certified to be the truth, the whole truth, and nothing but the truth, by Hartford VanDyke, a non-union non-Bar Association lawyer; NOT AN ATTORNEY!

Commerical Law Applied

9

IRS Personnel

Internal Revenue Service Personnel have no authority to levy salaries and wages from privately owned companies.

IRS authority is applicable solely to **government agencies and personnel** by 26 U.S.C. 6331(a):

"Levy may be made upon the accrued salary or wages of any **officer, employee, or elected official, of the United States,** the District of Columbia, or any agency or instrumentality of the United States or the District of Columbia, by serving **a notice of levy on the employer.**"

First, such notices must include a **Form 668B**, which is the actual levy.

Second, only those large businesses and governmental units that have designated officers and written agreements are authorized to receive **Notices of Levy** by mail.

Third, to complete the levy, another form, **Form 668C,** must be served, but cannot be served by mail; it must be served in person. That completes **service of "notice of levy".**

Absent **Form 668B** there is no evidence that there is a levy. In the event the IRS fails to serve **either or both the levy and Form 668C,** service of process is incomplete and the IRS defaults.

In brief, **there can be no seizure before a judgment in a state court is rendered.**

Further, the AGO (Attorney General's Office) states clearly that there are **two forms of judicial process** referred to above, **writs of attachment** and **writs of garnishment.**

And since **a notice of levy is neither,** it should be obvious that it is not **"service of process"** in any legal sense what-soever. **Federal law says that a levy is (must be) served with a writ of attachment.** Writs of attachment have a different purpose than writs of garnishment.

A levy is not a garnishment; a levy is an <u>attachment</u>.

It takes a court action to compel anyone to surrender a consumer's property to another (such as the IRS collection agency) **without the consumer's consent and over his objection.**

In sum, a "<u>notice of levy</u>" is not a levy nor a garnishment.

10
Lawful Status of the IRS

This Chapter is presented to expose the criminal conduct of the IRS regarding the racketerring activity of **Interference with Commerce** (18 USC 1951), **Extortionate Credit Transactions** (18 USC 891-894), and **Conspiracy against rights** (18 USC 241).

The **INTERNAL REVENUE SERVICE** has been informed of the law but they refuse to comply by unlawfully imposing **Notices of Levy** on the private income of consumers without due process of law.

The United States Code clearly establishes **"Due Process for Collections"** (26 USC 6330).

The common practice of this **Organized Crime** is clear, one office of the IRS accepts payment in full, then another office of the IRS levies against the property of that person and collects the debt yet again without any due process of law.

LAWFUL STATUS:

The INTERNAL REVENUE SERVICE is incorporated in Delaware as a collection agency for a Puerto Rico Company titled **INTERNAL REVENUE TAX AND AUDIT SERVICE (IRS)** /// For Profit General Corporation /// Incorporated date 7/12/33 /// File No. 0325720.

Therefore, the **INTERNAL REVENUE SERVICE** must be recognized in its lawful status as a **Collection Agency**; not fraudulently accepted as a **government agency**.

This business **Corporation** is accountable under **Title 15** of the **USC Section 1692e.**

A debt collector may not use false, deceptive or misleading representation.

It is a common misconception that the **INTERNAL REVENUE SERVICE** is part of the United States Government, but in fact, it is a **Private Corporation.**

Through fraud, manipulation, conspiracy, deceit, and impersonation of law enforcement personnel, the IRS has become an **Organized Crime Syndicate** operating illegally in every State of this union.

There are **three major elements** of this Organized Crime, as follows:

1. Extortionate Credit Transactions (18 USC 891-894).

This is the common practice of "IRS Agents" to threaten, coerce, intimidate and force the people to pay a "Debt" that the IRS fabricates out of thin air and can not lawfully establish. There is no due process of law allowed. Those who oppose the tax are prosecuted by US Attorneys who are more than willing to engage in **Conspiracy Against Rights** (18 USC 241) for the profits they receive from the money they **Extort** within the Fraud (18 USC 1001) of claiming to collect a debt that is owed.

Whereas, in fact, **no debt to the IRS can be lawfully established.** It cannot be lawfully established that an **American Citizen** owes this corporation anything, all claims that they do are **Fraud.**

2. Seizure of Property without Due Process — Violation of 4th Amendment.

It has become the common practice of the IRS to file **Levies** against Personal property without any judicial process. These levies are filed with the **Recorder of Deeds** who has established the common practice of allowing **levies**, of the IRS, to be recorded without a **Judgment signed by the judge**, lawfully required for the filing of a levy (26 USC 6330). Later, the **Agent** returns to the **Recorder of Deeds** and obtains a certified copy of the alleged **Lien** that they present to the Sheriff for seizure of the property. The Sheriffs and Deputies are duped into enforcing this bogus lien and violating the **American Citizen** without due process of law in violation of **the 4th Amendment**. It is the responsibility of every Sheriff to not enforce any levy not supported by a **Judgment signed by a Judge**. Every Sheriff has denied due process of law in every instance he has exercised a levy without judgment of the court.

3. Seizure of bank accounts/income without Due Process — Violation of 4th Amendment.

It has become the common practice of the IRS to seize bank accounts and income of the "American Citizens" without any due process of law. As clearly evident by the attached letter the IRS has taken $133.20 from David Anderson who was not informed or given the right to respond, because he would have "Disputed" the debt, because the debt has been paid in full. The IRS claims they have rights to property of private citizens and enforce those rights without judicial process. Thus, establishing "Organized Crime" for profit.

Lawful Challenge To The Secretary of the Treasury for the united States of America:

As clearly indicated the IRS is fraudulently operating under the designation of the **DEPARTMENT OF THE**

TREASURY. As a corporation, the IRS can not lawfully misrepresent itself to the public by declaring itself **to be a part of the US government.** This act is prohibited by **15 USC 1692e.**

Unless the **Secretary of the Treasury for the United States of America** is willing to state under **Penalty of Perjury** that he has given **Government Authority** to the IRS, a private for profit corporation, and willing to accept accountability for all acts of illegal seizure by the corporation. The IRS is clearly engaged in **conspiracy to defraud the public** by leading the public to believe they are **a part of the US government.**

This deception is being supported by the **US Department of the Treasury** clearly shown in the attached letter, by this government acting on behalf of the IRS without any due process of law. Either the **Secretary** will confirm or deny the IRS's government status and our **Representatives** must take action accordingly.

Our **United States Representatives** are responsible to stop this **Organized Crime** and to date have remained silent. The people have the right of protection of law and the systems being operated by the IRS are clearly a **deprivation** of **due process of law**. When criminals are engaged in **Organized Crime** and doing so under fraudulent authority by declaring themselves government, when in fact they are not, they are causing the people to despise their government and judge it by the conduct of the IRS Agents.

All IRS Agents are lawfully challenged as **Foreign Agents** under **22 USC 611**. They have no authority of law other than that of a debt collector under Title 15 of the United States Code. Either our current Representatives will remove the unlawful conduct of the IRS, or we must **Impeach** that

Representative and replace him with a **Representative** who will perform the duties of that **Public Office** in accordance with law.

IRS **Agents** are all enemies of the people. Giving IRS **Agents** aid and comfort establishes the crime of **Treason.**

All **Civil Officers** are subject to **Impeachment** for this crime under **Article II, Section 4** of the **Constitution for the united States of America.** Felony crimes are being reported to our **Representatives.**

Refusal to inform the proper authorities is the crime of **Misprision of Felony, 18 USC 4.**

"Whoever, **having knowledge of the actual commission of a felony cognizable by a court of the United States,** conceals and does not as soon as possible *make known the same* to some judge or other person in civil or military authority under the United States, shall be fined under this title or imprisoned not more than three years, or both."

Commerical Law Applied

11
Debt Validation

Debt Validation - The Ultimate Weapon Against the Collection Agencies

If a collection account comes into your life, you've heard about it in one of three ways:

1. It came up as a listing on your credit report, or
2. You received a telephone call from a collection agency,
3. You got a letter in the mail.

You could try to settle the debt with a collection agency, but you might want to try **debt validation** **first.**

The best defense against debt collectors is often debt validation. Why? Because **the collection agency may not even be legally entitled to collect the debt from you.**

YOU, JOE, BOB, & MONEY BORROWED

Let's say you borrowed money from your friend Joe. Joe would be the *creditor of this debt*, the original creditor. And, let's say time has gone by and you think you might still owe Joe money, although you're not sure how much.

One day, a guy named Bob comes up to you and says that he is collecting the money that you owe Joe. Bob is acting just like a collection agency for a credit card company would act. Think about it - having never met Bob before, would you just hand over your cash to him? No. Or at least I hope you would not. You should have these questions in mind to ask Bob:

legal document exists to prove that Bob is legally orized to collect money for Joe?

How much is the actual debt?

What payments have already been made on the account?

Where is the accounting of the debt, including all interest and fees?

Are these fees and interest amounts legitimate?

Do I really owe Joe the money?

You remember borrowing money from your friend Sam, at the same time. You remember paying one of them back the next day.

Is this the debt you borrowed from Sam or from Joe?

Where is the contract showing the terms of the loan with Joe and the contract with Sam?

At the very minimum you should phone Joe or Sam to ask about the loan.

You should have the same thoughts about a collection agency who sends you a bill for a debt you that may or may not owe.

Don't Panic

If you receive a phone call or a letter from a collection agency, your first reaction may be to panic. Calm down and think about the situation. Ignore all of the fancy language and legal terms that the collection agency uses to collect.

Think of what questions you would ask Bob in our example. If you do, you'll know exactly what to ask a collection agency (Bob in our example) to validate an alleged debt.

The Fair Debt Collection Practices Act

Debt Validation is a legal procedure which is spelled out by the Fair Debt Collection Practices Act, or FDCPA.

It matters if the alleged claim is from the original creditor (Joe) or collection agency (Bob).

The FDCPA does not cover collection tactics used by original creditors (like credit card companies who issue credit cards). It only governs the actions of debt collectors (collection agencies). Let's look at the definition of these two groups as defined by the Fair Debt Collection Practices Act (FDCPA):

Title VIII - Debt Collection Practices - § 803. Definitions. [15 USC 1692a]

(4) The term "creditor" means any person who offers or extends credit creating a debt or to whom a debt is owed, **but such term does not include any person that receives an assignment or transfer of a debt that is in default solely for the purpose of facilitating collection of such debt for another.**

This means that, as far as the FDCPA is concerned, *a creditor is the original entity which loaned money to a consumer. **The collection agency is _not_ the creditor.*** The definition of a debt collector is as follows:

(6) The term "debt collector" means any person who uses any instrumentality of interstate commerce or the mails in any business the principal purpose of which is the collection of any debts, or who regularly collects or attempts to collect, directly or indirectly, debts owed or due or asserted to be owed or due another.

So when a collection agency is assigned, or has purchased, your debt, they are NOT the creditor. **They are the debt collector** and the actions they take are all governed by the FDCPA.

What if the person asking you for the money (Bob) is a lawyer?

Under the FDCPA, even if Joe hires a law firm or lawyer to collect a debt from you, **the law firm of lawyer is still considered a collector** and must adhere to the FDCPA.

What does a debt collector need to provide as debt validation?

1 • Proof that the collection company owns the debt/or has been assigned the debt.

Bob is legally entitled to collect a debt he owns or has been assigned from you. This is basic contract law. It is very difficult to get a judgment without a direct contract between collection agency and the original creditor.

2 • At a minimum, some account statements from the original creditor.

You can pin them down on the amount of the debt by requiring complete payment history, starting with the original creditor. How did Bob calculate this alleged debt? What fees/interest has Bob tacked on, and how he determined these amounts? This requirement was established by the case · *Fields v. Wilber Law Firm, USCA-02-C-0072, 7th Circuit Court, Sept 2004.*

3 • Copy of the original wet ink signed loan agreement or credit card application.

Your contract with Joe establishing the debt between him and you. Account statements from the original date can fulfill these requirements.

What does Bob gets out of the deal?

It use to be, in most cases, that creditors **assigned**, not **sold**, its debts to a collection agency. But not any more.

Creditors hire collection companies (like Bob) to collect debts for them, because they simply don't have the time or resources to chase down all of their severely overdue accounts. Collection agencies maintain cheap labor and a streamlined system to pursue such accounts.

When a creditor hires a collection agency, the debt has been **assigned** to the collection agency. If a collection agency is successful at collecting the money on the account, they usually keep a percentage of what is collected as payment for services.

Original creditors sometimes sell debts in large portfolios to collection agencies. This is starting to be the norm, and several of these companies, called Junk Debt Buyers (JDBs), are now being traded on Wall Street. The companies do not spend much money for these debts, sometimes paying less than (1) cent on the dollar. Even if the debt is not a large debt, they often hire attorneys to send out mass form-letters to debtors in the hopes of collecting. As you can see, even if they get a small percentage of the debtors to pay, profits can be enormous.

Assigned or purchased debt. How do you know Bob is the right guy to pay?

Why should you care if a debt is purchased or assigned? In an **assignment**, the collection agency does not own the debt, and therefore you do not technically owe them any money. There is no way for a collection agency to prove that you owe them money because there is only an assignment of the debt and not a contract between you and the creditor.

One loophole: Some contracts have the wording *"debtor agrees to be responsible for payment of this debt to creditor OR ITS ASSIGNS."* This IS a contract between you and the debt collector as well as the creditor and if they can provide you with a copy of a contract that states this (with your wet ink signature!), you are pretty much stuck and need to negotiate the debt.

What if the collection agency (Bob) proves they purchased the debt? Is he now the original creditor and no longer subject to the FDCPA?

If they do purchase the debt, this does not make them the original creditor. They are still a debt collector covered by the FDCPA.

Continue to treat any collection agency, junk debt buyer or law firm who says they own the debt as a collection agency subject to the FDCPA. You can still request validation and proof of the purchase, because if they can't validate it, the collection agency can't prove you owe the debt. Often a JDB will lie telling a consumer that since they purchased the debt, they are not subject the the FDCPA. This simply not true.

The Right to Validate Your Debt

Under the FDCPA, you are allowed to validate this debt, and the creditor (in this case, the collection agency) must show you proof that you owe the debt to the collection agency (not to the original creditor.)

Section 809. Validation of debts [15 USC 1692g]

(b) If the consumer notifies the debt collector in writing within the thirty-day period described in subsection (a) that the debt, or any portion thereof, is disputed, or that the consumer requests the name and address of the original

creditor, the debt collector shall cease collection of
or any disputed portion thereof, until the debt
obtains verification of the debt or any copy of a judg
the name and address of the original creditor, and a copy or
such verification or judgment, or name and address of the
original creditor, is mailed to the consumer by the debt
collector.

They also must show <u>positive proof</u> that you owe them
this debt. It's not enough to send you a computer-generated
printout of the debt.

So, if a creditor can't validate a debt:
• They are not allowed to collect the debt,
• They are not allowed to contact you about the debt, and
• They are **not allowed to report it** under the <u>Fair Credit
Reporting Act</u> (FCRA). Doing so is a violation of the FCRA,
and the FCRA states that you can sue for $1,000 in
damages for any violation of the Act.

An opinion letter of the FTC clearly spells out that a
collection agency CANNOT report a debt to the credit
bureaus which has not been validated:

http://www.ftc.gov/os/statutes/fdcpa/letters/cass.htm

The opinion letter also states that you can sue in federal
or state court. So if you have them on a violation, then you
have damages of $1,000 for the incident plus damages.
<u>Small claims court, anyone</u>?

**What to do if a collection agency responds to your
request for validation with a summons to appear**

Some collection agencies are starting to respond to
validation requests with summons to appear in court.
Precedent has been established that <u>a collection agency
cannot file suit against you if they haven't validated the debt</u>

within the initial 30 day period. If this happens to you, you may cite the case: *Spears vs. Brennan*

The appeals court determined:

"[Plaintiff] Brennan (collection agency attorney) violated **15 U.S.C. § 1692g(b)** when he obtained a default judgment against [defendant] Spears after Spears had notified Brennan in writing that the debt was being disputed — before Brennan had mailed verification of the debt to Spears."

This means that you have an <u>absolute defense</u> in court to deny them judgment if they still have not validated the debt. Once you get your FDCPA dispute letter in, the collector cannot even get a judgment until they satisfy the FDCPA law. The appeals court overturned the <u>default summary judgment</u> in part because the collection agency lawyer did not meet the rules of the FDCPA.

This could be grounds for getting a default judgment vacated. It's also another violation of the FDCPA and you can collect $1,000 per incident from them.

12
Debt Validation in seven steps

Are collection agencies harassing you with repeated calls? Are you sure they're legally entitled to collect the debt? Before you make a payment, find out if the collection agency has the right to collect the alleged debt. This is where debt validation can help you out. Check the topics given below if you want to know what debt validation is all about.

What is validation of debt?

Debt validation is where you try to find out whether the collection agency (CA) has the legal right to collect on the debt by asking them to provide you with proof of claim.

The FDCPA (Fair Debt Collection Practices Act) gives you the right to seek validation from a collection agency that is not the original creditor. The FDCPA does not govern collection practices of original creditors.

Is there a time limit for validation of debt?

Under the FDCPA, debt collectors (collection agencies or CAs (collection agents)) are required to send you a debt validation notice within 5 days of contacting you to collect a debt. The notice informs you that you have the right to validate/dispute the debt within 30 days of receiving the letter. If you don't dispute the debt (or request validation of the debt) within the 30-day period, the collector has the legal right to assume that you agree the debt is valid.

What details do you get with debt validation?

When you try to validate a debt, the collection agency must provide you with certain details. They are:

1 • **Proof that the CA holds (owns) your debt:** You must get written proof that your account has been sold or assigned to the CA.

2 • **Your payment history:** You'll also get a copy of your current account payment history. This will help you verify the total amount you owe, including any fees being added to your debt. You should also find out how the CA has calculated these extra fees.

3 • **Copy of your original contract:** This is intended to prove to you that you agreed to the debt. If they do not provide you with a copy of the original agreement, the CA may also provide you with the account statements from the original creditor instead.

What are the steps in validation of debt?

Check out these 7 steps to validate your debt and deal with collectors and credit reporting agencies (CRAs).

1 • **Request a validation:** Send a request letter to the CA asking them to validate your debt. Check out this sample debt validation letter (page XX) to learn how to format the letter. The letter should be sent via certified mail with a return receipt request.

2 • **Check if the CA is licensed:** You need to wait for a reply from the CA. The agency may send you a letter with the details you've asked for. While you wait for a response, you should check to see if your state requires CAs to be licensed, and if so, whether the CA you are dealing with is licensed. The states that do not require CA licensing are Georgia, California, Iowa, Kansas, Kentucky, Montana,

Oklahoma, Pennsylvania, and South Carolina.

3 • **What if the CA violates collection laws:** If the collector needs a license to collect debt in your state and they aren't licensed, send them a letter notifying they are violating your state's collection law. You should also inform them that if they continue to attempt collection, they may be facing a law suit and pay fines to your state.

4 • **What to do if the CA doesn't validate debt:** If the CA doesn't send you satisfactory proof, then you need to send them the documents below:

- A copy of your validation demand letter.
- Copy of the postal return receipt..
- A statement that the CA has violated the FDCPA.

Under the FDCPA, if the collection agency doesn't validate your debt, then they can no longer collect the payment and they are required to stop contacting you.

5 • **Remove collection listing:** Under the FCRA, collection agencies should not report a negative entry to the CRAs (Credot Reporting Agencies) if the CA does not validate your debt. Send a letter to the collection agency asking them to remove the collection listing. Also inform them that if they don't remove the collection listing, you might sue them for violation of the FDCPA. Wait 15-20 days for a reply from the collector. They'll either remove the negative listing or they won't respond at all.

6 • **Sue the collector if listing isn't removed:** If the collectors don't remove the collection listing from your report, then you can file a lawsuit because they have violated the FDCPA. Before you file the lawsuit inform the CRAs that the CA is refusing to remove the collection listing.

7 • **Know how to deal with the CRAs:** If the CRAs verify the collection listing, you'll have verification that the

CA has the right to collect on the debt. If the CRA validates the debt, you should send them proof that the CA has refused to respond to your attempts to validate the debt, and therefore is violating the FDCPA. If the CRA refuses to send you the validation information they have received from the CA, you should include them in your suit against the CA for violation of the FDCPA.

Can you dispute the debt after validation period?
You can send in a **validation letter** to your CA after the 30-day period, but the collectors aren't legally obligated to reply or stop collection efforts. So, you shouldn't dispute debt after the validation period has expired.

Debt assigned to CA - how does it affect validation?
If your debt is assigned to a CA, they may not be the legal owner of the debt. Sometimes if a debt has been assigned to a CA, it means they have purchased the account from the original creditor and sometimes it means that the creditor has hired the CA to collect the debt for them. When you validate the debt, you should find out how the CA and the original creditor are connected and who has the power to agree to a settlement or payment plan.

How do validation and debt verification differ?
If they validate the debt, the collector is required to send a copy of your agreement with the original creditor. If you are trying debt verification, the collector only needs to provide you with a written statement with the name and address of the original creditor and the total amount you owe. The time you have to verify a debt is similar to the time you have to validate the debt.

Under the FDCPA, CAs must stop collection activities as soon as they receive your request for validation or verification within the 30-day period. They can resume collection efforts only after they've sent you satisfactory proof that you owe the debt.

With debt validation, you can avoid harassment by collection agencies by verifying whether you legally owe the money. Once the CA verifies your debt, it is easier for you to plan how to pay back the money you owe. Always be sure you know and enforce your rights if the CA refuses to validate or verify the debt.

Commerical Law Applied

13
Debt Validation Strategy

Dispute the collection with the credit bureaus.

Look up the **Statute of Limitations** (SOL) on the debt. If the debt is past the statute of limitations, send them a letter informing that they are trying to collect "**zombie debt**". This is debt which is too old to have any legal liabilty for a consumer. Here is a **sample letter** for this.

If the collection agency does not remove the listing after you point out the SOL, sometimes your only remedy is to sue them.

If the debt is not past the statute of limitations, send a **letter requesting validation** to the collection agency (our buddy Bob in the preceding example). If you don't know the address of the collection agency, **here is a tip** to help you find it.

Wait 30 days to hear back from the collection agency. Most likely they will not respond; or they will respond saying that they received your letter, but only with one of the following; not all three:

• Proof that the collection company owns the debt/or has been assigned the debt.

• Copies of statements from the original creditor.

• Copy of the original wet ink signed loan agreement or credit card application.

If they haven't sent you satisfactory proof, and are still reporting this on your report, send a copy of your receipt for your registered mail, a copy of the first letter you sent and a statement that they have not complied with the **FDCPA** and e now in violation of the Act. Tell them they need to immediately remove the collection listing from your credit report or you are going to **file a lawsuit** against them because they would also be in violation of the FDCPA, section 809 (b).

Wait 15-20 days to hear back after this second letter to the collection agency. They will either remove it or not respond.

If they do provide a contract with a signature from the original creditor showing that you owe the debt, there is one more thing you can do: <u>see if they are legally licensed to collect the debt in your state</u>.

If you believe that they are not licensed, and licensing is required in your state, write them another letter and <u>tell them they are in violation of your state's collection laws and are subject to prosecution and fines</u>. Cite your state's fines and procedures in the letter. <u>This is a last ditch effort, but has worked in some cases</u>.

Typically, your work will stop here, as most debt collection agencies will bow down to your demands and send you a letter agreeing to remove the listing. Now all you have to do is send a copy of the letter to the CRAs (Credit Reporting Agencies).

If the collection agency did not agree to remove the listing, then you need to continue to the next steps.

File a lawsuit in small claims court against the collection agency on the basis of violating the FDCPA.

Have the papers served to the collection agency. (You can find a paper server on the internet for about $25). Here is a good link:

http://www.1-800-serve-em.com/servicemap.html

In the meantime, in a parallel effort with your **lawsuit against the collection agency**.

If the collection comes back as "verified" from the credit bureaus, you now have proof of further collection activity from the collection agency. (The assumption is that the credit bureau contacted the collection agency to verify the debt.) Since the collection agency did not validate the debt, further collection activity is a violation of the FDCPA.

Contact the credit bureaus, and tell them that the creditors did not verify the debts under the **FDCPA**, and send copies of your proof. Request the **method of verification**, which is your right under the FCRA. It is crucial to contact the credit bureaus before filing a lawsuit. Make sure you state that the collection agency did not respond to your request for debt validation.

You can try sending them **this letter** to see if they will budge. They may tell you that the request needs to come from the creditor. This is baloney. If they can't give you reasonable information on how they verified the information and the collection agency has provided you none, you can conclude there was no reasonable investigation performed. They are teetering on the edge of "willful non-compliance" under the FCRA. Tell them so.

File a suit in either small claims, state or federal court. The basis of the lawsuit should be that the credit bureaus could not provide a satisfactory method of verification, or did not conduct a reasonable investigation.

Have the papers served. (You can find a paper server on the internet for about $25). Here is a great link where you can search for the local office of the credit bureau near you.

http://www.llrx.com/columns/roundup14.htm

Notify the bureaus that you are suing them. You can use this letter. The credit bureaus will call the creditors and find out that there is a question about whether the debt is legitimate. They should delete it immediately. If you want more legal ammo, you might also try looking up similar cases to cite. We have a list of online legal resources.

I hope these tips have encouraged you. Good luck on pursuing financial freedom!

13
Sample Letter requesting validation of debt

Under the **FDCPA**, you have the right to ask for validity of the debt that the collection agency says you owe to them.

You'll need the Debt Validation Letter in order to challenge the validity of the alleged debt.

Given below is a sample debt validation letter for you to understand how to request in writing for **validation of debt.**

Your Name
Your Address
Your City, State & Zip
Your Phone #

Date

Creditor's Name
Department
Creditor's Address
Creditor's City, State & Zip

Re: _____Acount Number_____

Dear Sir or Madam,

This is to inform you that I recently pulled my credit report and noticed that there's a collection listing from your agency on my credit report. I have never been notified of this collection action or that I owed the debt. This letter is to inform you that I would like to have a verification of the debt and your ability to collect this money from me.

Under the FDCPA, I have the right to request a validation of this debt. I request that you prove that I am indeed the party who is contractually obligated to pay off this debt.

Please be aware that reporting any invalidated information to major credit bureaus may constitute defamation of character. In addition, also be aware that until you validate this debt, you cannot continue collection activities or report this information to the credit bureaus. Non-compliance with this request may place your company in serious legal trouble with the Federal Trade Commission (FTC) and other state/federal agencies.

Please attach copies of the following documents:

Agreement with your client that authorizes you to collect on this alleged debt.

Agreement that bears signature of the alleged debtor where he promises to pay the original creditor.

Complete payment history on this account, to prove that the amount you wish to collect is accurate.

Sincerely,

Your Signature
Your Name

*"The wicked man does deceptive work.
But to him who sows righteousness will be
a sure reward.*

Proverbs 11:18

Commerical Law Applied

It is presumptuous, irresponsible, and a violation of due process of law to cite a section from a Code that is not enacted into positive law.

Examples of Titles of the US Code that are NOT enacted in positive law include:

Title 26: Internal Revenue Code

[1 USC § 204]

Commerical Law Applied

Other Publications

1. **Nesara I**
   https://www.createspace.com/3676730
2. **Nesara II**
   https://www.createspace.com/3694967
3. **Be The One**
   https://www.createspace.com/3921716
4. **Commercial Redemption**
   https://www.createspace.com/3397150
5. **Hardcore Redemption-in-Law**
   https://www.createspace.com/3475497
6. **Commercial Law Applied**
   https://www.createspace.com/3960715
7. **The Matrix As It Is**
   https://www.createspace.com/3495158
8. **Give Yourself Credit**
   https://www.createspace.com/3462990
9. **From Debt To Prosperity**
   https://www.createspace.com/3485734
10. **DebtOcracy**
    https://www.createspace.com/3650756
11. **Asset Protection**
    https://www.createspace.com/3700522
12. **Untold History Of America**
    https://www.createspace.com/3407070
13. **New Beginning Study Course**
    https://www.createspace.com/3412422
14. **Reclaim Your Sovereignty**
    https://www.createspace.com/3418256
15. **Oil Beneath Our Feet**
    https://www.createspace.com/3420496
16. **The People's Voice**
    https://www.createspace.com/3724222
17. **My Home Is My Castle**
    https://www.createspace.com/3464566
18. **Maine Street Miracle**
    https://www.createspace.com/3397262

CPSIA information can be obtained
at www.ICGtesting.com
Printed in the USA
LVHW082335270519
619236LV00028B/526/P